GOURMET PRESERVES

Chez Madelaine

Delicious marmalades, jams, jellies, and preserves
to make at home—plus easy muffins, scones,
crêpes, puddings, pastries, desserts, and breakfast
treats to serve with them.

Madelaine Bullwinkel

**SURREY
BOOKS
Chicago**

GOURMET PRESERVES CHEZ MADELAINE is published by
Surrey Books, Inc., 230 E. Ohio St., Suite 120, Chicago, IL 60611.

First edition: 1 2 3 4 5

This book is manufactured in the United States of America

Library of Congress Cataloging-in-Publication Data

Bullwinkel, Madelaine.
    Gourmet preserves Chez Madelaine : delicious marmalades, jams, jellies, and preserves to make at
home—plus easy muffins, scones, crêpes, puddings, pastries, desserts, and breakfast treats to serve
with them / Madelaine Bullwinkel. —1st ed.
      p. cm.
      Includes index.
      ISBN 1-57284-078-1
      1. Jam. 2. Jelly. I. Title.
      TX612.J3B8523 2005
      641.8'52—dc22
                    2004028507

Editorial services: Bookcrafters Inc.
Art direction, book design, and production: Joan Sommers Design, Chicago

For prices on quantity purchases or for free book catalog, contact Surrey Books
at the above address or at www.surreybooks.com

This title is distributed to the trade by Publishers Group West.

For my Mother, Mary Gaylord de Huszar, and George

CONTENTS

Introduction ix

1 A Short History of Preserving 1

2 Techniques and Equipment for Preserving 5

3 Jams 23

4 No-Sugar Jams 75

5 Jellies 93

6 Marmalades 113

7 Preserves 147

8 Breads and Muffins 183

9 Desserts 217

Appendix: A Seasonal Guide to Fresh Fruits
and Vegetables for Preserving 251

Index 257

INTRODUCTION

Rarely does a cooking teacher have the opportunity to share a long-time passion with a new generation of eager cooks and seasoned preservers alike. I don't think you will be disappointed. The recipes in *Gourmet Preserves Chez Madelaine* remain true to the traditional methods that first inspired me to make jams and jellies more than thirty years ago. At the same time, they keep pace with both cooking trends and technical preserving advances in the 21st century. Each recipe has evolved slowly and naturally over years of testing, sampling, and enjoying at Chez Madelaine, my home-based cooking school.

Gourmet Preserves is really two books in one. If you are new to fruit preserving, the second chapter will read like an owner's manual. A list of instructions also accompanies each preserving subject in the chapters that follow. But, trust me, once you have the basic techniques mastered, the process of cooking preserves will become both predictable and fun. Additional rewards await you in the baking and dessert sections—those recipes provide an opportunity to amplify delicious home-made treats with your personally created preserves. Don't even try to resist!

Gourmet Preserves captures, in its technical efficiency, the spirit of new approaches to fruit preserving. For instance, careful experimentation over the years has led me to develop recipes for small fruit quantities—often appropriate for limited family needs—that preserve full flavor with a minimum of cooking and adhere to natural pectin levels, which means less added sugar. We now vacuum seal all preserves, in keeping with standards of the preserving industry, which has discarded melted paraffin as both unreliable and flammable. All our breads are now checked for doneness with a modern, instant-read thermometer, so we can say goodbye to the guesswork of thumping on hot loaves.

Look for some (to me) daring technical twists, such as the use of powdered commercial pectin; it helps make Quick Preserves and comes to the rescue when preserves refuse to jell. You will learn how to add just the right amount of pectin powder to keep sugar levels the same as they would be if you used only naturally occurring fruit pectin. Preserve connoisseurs will still prefer the texture and mouth-feel of natural pectin in jelly, preserves, and marmalades, but, like me, I think you will be grateful to have an alternative when time is limited.

What hasn't changed in the many years I have been making fruit preserves is the knowledge that each labeled jar is truly a present from the heart—from me, from my kitchen. There's no better gift nor way to say "thank you" to friends and associates. I make sure to pack several quarter-pint jars in my carry-on bag each time I lead a tour group to France, knowing that old friends will be looking forward to receiving these unique personal gifts as an expression of our common love of life at the table.

Now it's time for you to join with me in the pleasure and satisfaction of creating an abundance of elegant and delicious fruit preserves right in your own home kitchen. After you have tried your hand at fruit preserving, let me know how you have fared. Please send news of your successes, questions, and recipe creations to me at: *chezmpreserves.com*.

A SHORT HISTORY OF PRESERVING

THE FIRST PRESERVES

From the earliest times, out of sheer necessity, our ancestors preserved abundant harvests for later consumption. These pre-scientific forebears often saw their precious food supply succumb to decay from mold and bacteria, so they learned to freeze fruits, vegetables, meats, and fish in cold regions and air-dry them in hot, arid climates.

The Romans tried to preserve fresh figs, pears, and plums in honey, not realizing that raw produce can still decay from within in the absence of air. Evidence of the first cooked fruit preserved in sugar comes from the early years of the Italian Renaissance. The fruits are described in Boccaccio's fourteenth-century writing as luxurious fare for the aristocracy living a romantic lifestyle. At that time sugar was imported from the Near East through Venice; it remained rare and quite expensive through the eighteenth century.

THE SEARCH FOR CHEAP SUGAR

By the middle of the sixteenth century, translations of Italian cookbooks with recipes for preserves began to appear in France. The first instance of a *marmalet* in an English cookbook dates from the early 1500s. Its source was a Portuguese recipe for preserved *marmelo* quince. Sweet preserves graced the royal tables of Europe with increasing regularity as their popularity spread northward. When the New World was cultivated, sugar

1

became a staple crop, and preserves became part of the European legacy.

Many islands in the Caribbean grew generous sugar crops using slave labor. There were also good-sized sugar plantations in Louisiana, Alabama, Florida, Georgia, and Mississippi before the Civil War. But the sugar content of American crops was lower than that grown in the West Indies, so the United States imported cheap molasses from the islands to meet its sugar needs. Only in the mid-nineteenth century was an inexpensive method for processing cane sugar perfected. On the heels of this discovery came the burgeoning production of sugar from beets. Now many more households could afford to experience the pleasures of preserves.

THE VACUUM SEAL: A TIMELESS INVENTION

In 1810, in France, Nicholas Appert invented a method for canning in glass jars. But it took another century and the ingenuity of three Americans to bring a safe preserving vacuum-sealed jar to the home cook in America. John Mason first patented a glass jar with threaded top and airtight metal cap. The Ball brothers picked up Mason's designs when his patents expired and continued to make Mason's jars. In 1915 John Kerr bought the rights to a German heat-sealing gasket on a lacquered metal lid that would vent air when heated and then seal quickly when cooled. Today we buy Ball's version of the Mason jar with a Kerr screw cap lid.

This clever innovation coupled with the drop in sugar prices had a dramatic effect in the marketplace. It made fruit preserving accessible to homemakers. It also allowed for the safe and inexpensive manufacture of preserves on a large commercial scale. More and more people took advantage of the opportunity to purchase preserves, though homemade preserves continued to be a staple in rural communities and among those who carried on family cooking traditions.

PRESERVING TODAY

Early in the twentieth century, the natural jelling substance in fruit, called pectin, was isolated and processed for commercial preservers. Concentrated pectin in liquid and powdered form was also introduced to housewives as a foolproof way to make jellies, marmalades, and preserves. Now one could choose between natural pectin and processed pectin to achieve the jell.

In 1974 the sale of glass jars by the Ball Corporation rose dramatically. The people who had returned to home gardening in the early 1970s were learning to preserve the economy and honesty of their new cuisine for the winter. The rise in home preserving was, in part, symptomatic of a period of national self-scrutiny in America. We questioned the environmental quality of our cities, the use of pesticides in farming, and the presence of additives and chemical preservatives in processed foods.

The steady rise of organic agriculture in the last twenty years attests to America's continuing commitment to remove chemicals from our food supply and restore its full flavor through small-scale farming. Grocery chains specializing in organic produce are on the rise. Farmers' markets, once an urban oddity, have proliferated in cities and suburban areas throughout the country. We are gradually coming full circle toward restoring our right to a simpler quality of life, one now free from necessity and devoted to pleasure at the table.

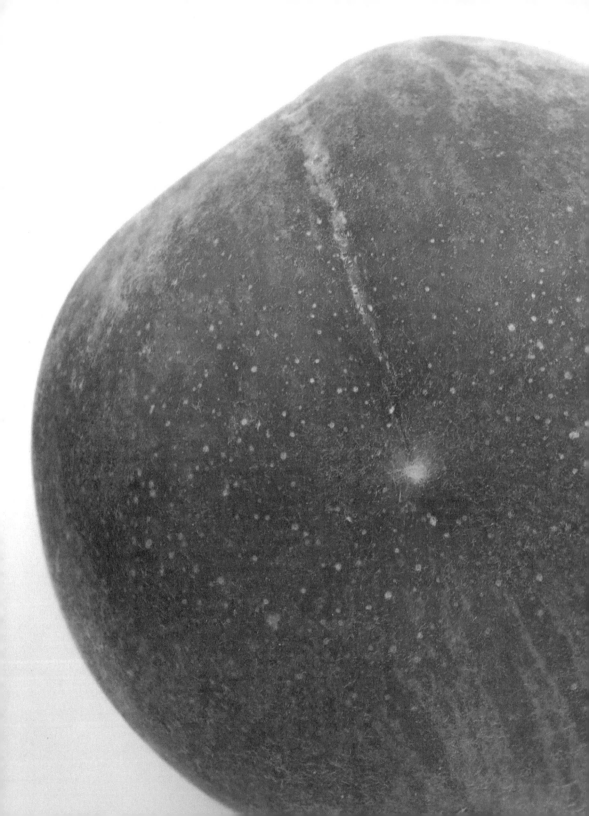

TECHNIQUES AND EQUIPMENT FOR PRESERVING

Whether you're new to fruit preserving or a veteran, this chapter is an essential review of basic definitions and a brisk walk-through of the process itself. There is the standard amount of repetition and ritual activity in preserving, but there's also some fascinating kitchen chemistry at work. We will go into detail to explain the "whys" that underlie the "how to's" of preserving because they are exciting when you are in the driver's seat. You may not be able to see the molecules as they jell, but if you appreciate the chemistry, you can make better decisions as you cook. Once you've mastered the art of the pectin jell, you can experiment with confidence.

DEFINITIONS OF JAM, JELLY, MARMALADE, AND PRESERVES

All the recipes in this book, aside from the baking and dessert chapters, are fruit preserves. Almost always, fruit is cooked with sugar to preserve its flavor and prevent spoilage. Our one exception is no-sugar jam, which relies simply on the fructose that is naturally present in fruit.

Several kinds of preserves rely on the jell:

- Jellies are jelled high-pectin fruit juices.
- Preserves are fruit pieces suspended in a fruit-juice jell.
- Marmalades are citrus fruits and peels jelled in their own juices.

Jams are usually not jells. This is the ideal technique for preserving low-pectin fruits. With jams, the adventurous cook can experiment with unusual fruit combinations and seasonings free from the technical considerations of the jell. However, fruits rich in pectin also cook easily and quickly into jelled jams. We don't call them preserves because they lack suspended fruit pieces. Their texture is more concentrated.

You can also make a jam without adding sugar. Unsweetened fruit juices provide the liquid medium for preserving fresh and dried fruits in no-sugar jams.

WHAT IS PECTIN AND HOW DOES IT FORM A JELL?

Pectin is a fibrous carbohydrate, bulging with entrapped water molecules. All fruits contain pectin when unripe, many retain some pectin when ripe, while others retain almost none. High levels of pectin are found in fruits such as apples, black and red currants, cranberries, blackberries, blueberries, and quinces. The citrus fruits—orange, grapefruit, lemon, and lime—carry pectin in their bitter peels. They are considered to have a good pectin level as do Concord grapes, plums, red raspberries, and strawberries. Fruits with low or negligible pectin content include apricots, cherries, figs, pears, peaches, pineapple, and rhubarb.

All fruits must be cooked for 10 minutes before the pectin is shaken loose enough to be measured easily. If a little acid is present in this heated solution, the pectin will also change its molecular structure and physical properties, becoming less possessive of its water and more attracted to other pectin molecules. The addition of sugar at this point causes a critical chemical reaction.

THE DIGITAL SCALE

Weighing fruits and berries is much easier with the recent introduction of the digital scale for the home kitchen. The footprint on the counter of this handy tool is that of a small notebook. This new generation of scale is accurate to a fraction of an ounce and can transform ounces into grams. Best of all, there is a reset button that compensates for the weight of a strainer or measuring cup and allows the cook to weigh only the contents. It's the most efficient way to weigh small quantities of loose berries and large fruits as well.

In the presence of heat and acid, granulated sugar reverts to its simpler forms: glucose and fructose. These sugars hungrily strip water molecules off the pectin chains. The unfettered pectin strands then come together freely. This dense web of pectin that holds and supports the aqueous sugars is a jell.

HOW TO MEASURE THE PECTIN LEVEL IN FRUIT

Performing the test for pectin is an optional exercise if you simply follow the recipes in *Gourmet Preserves*. The ingredients have all been measured to assure the proper pectin level and sugar requirement. This pectin test is essential only if you wish to experiment with an original recipe using the jell. And curious cooks will find that measuring pectin fulfills the irresistible desire to actually see what is normally invisible in the saucepan. It assures one of complete control in a preserve recipe.

To perform the pectin test, stir 1 tablespoon of unsweetened, cooked fruit juice at room temperature into a small, shallow bowl away from a heat source. Stir in 1 to 1 1/2 tablespoons of grain alcohol (available at liquor stores) or rubbing alcohol, and let this combination stand for one minute.

When you pour the mixture out on a plate, clear, congealed pectin lumps will appear. The larger the lumps the higher the pectin content. To fully evaluate the pectin level in each test, pick up the pectin pieces on a fork. The highest pectin level will form a solid mass on the tines. Equally acceptable levels of pectin will produce heavy strands. If the pectin masses are unrelated small lumps or ripples that don't cling to the fork, then pectin level is low. Reducing the juices or adding pectin-rich juice will be necessary to create a jell.

Immediately throw out the alcohol solution without tasting it after each test. Grain alcohol is 90 percent alcohol and rubbing alcohol is toxic. They are also flammable and should be stored in a cool place.

FRUITS WITH HIGH PECTIN LEVELS
Blackberry
Black Currant
Black Raspberry
Blueberry
Concord Grape
Crabapple
Cranberry
Green Apple
Quince
Red Currant
Serviceberry

FRUITS WITH GOOD PECTIN LEVELS
Grapefruit
Lemon
Lime
Orange
Plum
Red Raspberry
Strawberry

FRUITS WITH LOW PECTIN LEVELS
Apricot
Cherry
Fig
Kiwifruit
Nectarine
Peach
Pear
Rhubarb
Pineapple

Testing for Pectin

Stir one tablespoon of fruit juice into one and one-half tablespoons of grain alcohol.

After one minute, pour the mixture onto a plate.

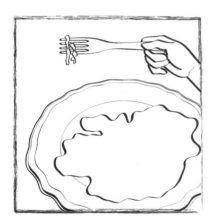

Connected strands indicate good pectin content. Reduce juices by one-half before adding sugar.

Coherent masses of pectin indicate excellent jelling potential. Use sugar cup for cup with juice.

HOW TO RAISE THE PECTIN LEVEL FOR THE JELL

Only fruits and berries with the highest pectin levels produce cooked juices with sufficient pectin to jell directly. One easy strategy to help assure optimal level in all fruit juices is to include 20 percent under-ripe fruit. These slightly green fruits and berries also have a desirable amount of acid that acts as a catalyst in the jelling process.

Recipes that combine fruits with differing pectin levels, such as Strawberry Blackberry Preserves and Orange Cranberry Marmalade, exemplify another technique for raising pectin levels naturally. They also suggest the synergetic potential of mingled fruit flavors. Pectin itself is generic; it accumulates.

When the inclusion of under-ripe fruit or the addition of high-pectin fruit are not sufficient to produce the desired pectin level, a more dramatic alternative is to reduce the fruit juices and concentrate the pectin. You will find that some recipes in the jelly chapter call for reducing fruit juices by as much as half their volume for this purpose.

In recipes for the most delicate wine jellies or quick-jelled preserves, none of the above techniques will be adequate to the task of producing an adequate pectin level for the jell. We offer two choices for the home preserver.

1) My preferred solution is the addition of Apple Pectin Stock made from Granny Smith apples. (A useful byproduct of making Apple Pectin Stock is the apple pulp that remains in the strainer. Once passed through a food mill to remove skins and pips, apple puree can be added to breads, muffins, pancakes, and waffles with delicious results. Check the index for specific recipes. Apple Pectin Stock keeps for up to a month well refrigerated.)

POTS FOR STERILIZING JARS

Select a large pot for sterilizing empty jars and vacuum-sealing no-sugar jams. My preferred vessel is an aluminum spaghetti pot with a slotted insert that holds the jars off the bottom so they don't bounce around during boiling. A 12-quart stock pot that will accommodate a 10-inch round cake cooling rack in the bottom is my second choice.

CLEARING THE WATER

From time to time preserving jars will come out of the sterilizing pot with a gritty residue on their surface. This could be the work of paper debris from an unremoved label on a jar or mineral build-up in the water. The addition of a tablespoon of distilled vinegar per quart of water will precipitate these materials to the bottom and clear the water. Replace the water bath with fresh water at the next opportunity.

2) The use of powdered commercial pectin is the other solution. Used in judicious amounts, commercial pectin need not require the use of more sugar than is used in recipes that rely on a natural level of pectin. Recipes entitled Quick Preserves call for one tablespoon Sure-Jell® for each cup of low-pectin fruit juice. This addition produces a jell without the need to reduce juices. (In my opinion, the texture produced with commercial pectin has a heavier consistency and a somewhat gummy mouth feel. However, the flavors remain true, and the benefit of speedy execution occasionally outweighs these textural shortcomings.)

MEASURING SUGAR AND ACID FOR THE JELL

Once the proper pectin level is achieved, the formula for creating the jell falls into place. Every cup of juice requires a cup of sugar to form a jell. The acid level is important, too. I ask you to add 1 tablespoon of freshly squeezed juice per cup of juice. Even when the chemistry does not require this much acid, I still add it to complement and balance the fruit flavors in a preserve.

The beauty of working with exacting pectin levels is that it takes little time, only 5 to 10 minutes, for a preserve to reach jell stage. Preserves cooked longer take on the darkened appearance and gooey consistency of caramelizing sugar. Not only does quick jelling preserve fruit flavor but it's also a matter of pride to have technical control. These are the two reasons we prefer our homemade preserves to store-bought brands.

MEASURING UTENSILS

Measuring utensils are calibrated for specific uses. Pyrex glass measures are designed to hold liquids while metal cups and spoons are sized for dry ingredients. The home preserver will want glass measures in pint, quart, and two-quart sizes. A set of nesting metal cup measures and teaspoon to tablespoon measures are also essential.

GETTING STARTED: STERILIZING PRESERVING JARS

Even before handling the fruit, the fruit preserver prepares the jars that will hold and seal the finished product. These need to be sterilized, a procedure that can take place, without supervision, at the same time as the cooking process.

Sterilizing is a simple routine that can be easily repeated in even the smallest of kitchens. This step is important, as it allows for the quick sealing of preserves once jars are closed. In other words, planning ahead will save you time later

Fill a large 8-quart pot—a pasta pot with a slotted insert is perfect or a deep pan fitted with a cake rack—with 4 quarts of cool water. Submerge as many new or clean, quilted preserving jars as the recipe requires. Cover the pot and bring the water to a boil. Simmer the empty jars for 15 minutes to sterilize them. *Note:* The lids will be sterilized later, and the screw caps need only to be clean, not sterilized.

At the same time, set aside a cooling rack near the range, first to drain the empty jars and then to cool the filled jars. Set out new lids, screw caps for sealing the jars, and a clean towel. Other important equipment are a funnel for filling the jars without spillage and a candy thermometer for measuring the jell. Tongs, a jar lifter, and oven mitts are also necessities for handling the hot jars.

KNIVES

A small collection of sharpened, high-quality knives helps make fruit preparation a pleasurable task. A large chef's knife will aid in cutting up apples, pineapples, and citrus fruits. A paring knife is a more comfortable size when working with small fruits and berries. A finely serrated tomato knife gives the preserver excellent control when thinly slicing unpeeled citrus fruits and tough-skinned plums and tomatoes. If marmalade becomes your specialty, the purchase of a small bird's beak knife is a must. This small cutting tool has a curved blade that cuts off citrus peels with a single flick of the wrist.

PREPARING FRUIT FOR PRESERVING

Each of the recipes specifies fruit quantities by the pound or, in the case of larger fruits, by the piece, and sometimes by both. Rinsing is all that is required for berries and soft fruits. Organic, hard, and citrus fruits receive a scrubbing with a vegetable brush as well as a rinsing in cold water in my kitchen.

The unwanted skin of apples and pears is easily removed with a peeler or paring knife. Blanching in boiling water is the preferred method for removing the skin of soft fruits such as apricots, peaches, and tomatoes. This process involves dipping the fruit in boiling water for 30 seconds, then immediately

Select a heavy 5-quart
saucepan with heatproof
handles and lid for recipes
that call for 2 pounds of fruit.
An 8-quart pot is a more
comfortable size for larger
quantities and fruits that foam
up when boiled. Preferred
materials are coated aluminum
or ceramic-covered cast iron.
Stainless steel pans are
acceptable if they have a
heavy copper or nickel
coating on the bottom that
improves conductivity.

Thin metal pans are poor
preserving pans because they
are vulnerable to burning the
fragile fruit and sugar contents
over the hot flame required for
fruit preserving.

Uncoated aluminum pans are
also discouraged as containers
for fruit mixtures. The acidic
character of preserves strips off
aluminum oxide, a compound
that naturally forms on
untreated aluminum surfaces.
Although not toxic, its color
and flavor are undesirable in a
preserve. That is why all recipes
in *Gourmet Preserves* call for
non-reactive pans.

into an ice water bath to stop further cooking.
When the fruit is cool enough to handle, the
skins will slip off easily.

The peel of citrus fruits receives more attention than that of other fruits because it is the
source of high-quality pectin and fragrant
oils. Marmalade recipes will clearly specify
whether or not the superficial zest, deep
narrow strips, or whole peel of the citrus is
to be used. The important distinction to be
made here is between the outer peel, the
colored part, which contains the desirable oils,
and the spongy, white inner portion that is
rich in pectin but also quite bitter. In several
recipes some portion of the white portion
of the peel is wrapped in cheesecloth and
simmered in the liquid to extract its pectin.
It is then removed before sugar is added.

All fruits are sectioned, sliced, or chopped
into pieces roughly the same size. This helps
assure that preserves cook evenly and are
consistent in texture. I prefer to chop up
pineapple by hand with a sharp knife because
the texture of the cooked pieces has an
appealing mouth feel. If you do not enjoy
working by hand, a mandoline or food-slicer
is an alternative tool. A food processor is the
appliance of choice for chopping hard fruits
and unpeeled sections of citrus fruits.

THE COOKING PROCESS

Despite the history and romance associated
with the shallow copper preserving pot,
I prefer modern nonreactive pots and pans,
ranging in size from 4 to 8 quarts. Covering
the pot once the fruit is added allows the heat to build to a
simmer more quickly. Often a recipe will call for a small

amount of water to coat the bottom of the pan and prevent sticking early on. All fruits are cooked at least 10 minutes before sugar is added.

Lemon juice is added after the initial cooking period and before the sugar. When the sugar is added, it should enter slowly in half-cup amounts. The cook stirs it in and waits until the juices begin to boil again before adding more. In the jam recipes cooking continues until the cook is satisfied with the consistency. The preserves that jell take a slightly different course. The juice is separated from the fruit pulp after the initial cooking, and sugar is added to the juices. They will boil up with a vigor that cannot be stirred down. The candy thermometer goes into the pan at this point.

The jell point on the thermometer is 8 degrees above the boiling temperature of water, which is 212 degrees F. at sea level. If you are not at sea level, submerge the thermometer in several inches of boiling water to determine your boiling point, then add 8 degrees to establish your specific jell point. (Test any new thermometer this way, even if you live at sea level. Thermometers are not always calibrated precisely.) Hold the thermometer vertically and bend over to read the temperature at eye level with the column of mercury. Your preserve will not jell until the exact temperature is reached.

ARE WE THERE YET? TESTING FOR THE JELL

When the candy thermometer reaches about 216 degrees F. the jelling juices will begin to sheet off a spoon. To run this quick test, dip a large metal spoon in the bubbling preserve, fill it, then let the liquid pour off one side. If the juices collect

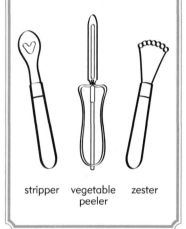
13

together and fall in a single drop or sheet, the jelly is nearing the jell point. This is a reassuring but not definitive sign of a jell.

The next test to run as the thermometer reaches 218 degrees involves a cold plate. (It helps to have planned ahead by placing a plate in the freezer.) A teaspoon of hot preserve on this chilled plate will cool quickly and jell. Return it to the freezer for a minute while the preserve continues boiling. Once cooled, the juices will hold their shape on the plate at the jell point. A finger run through juice without fruit will leave wrinkles in its wake.

The thermometer remains the most accurate test for the fruit jell. For accuracy, test the thermometer when new as indicated in the section above. View the mercury level at eye level. For added insurance, continue cooking the preserve that has reached the jell point for one minute.

ADDING HERBS, SPICES, AND LIQUORS TO PRESERVES

Once you gain confidence in your preserving skills, the imaginative addition of fresh herbs, spices, and liquors can greatly expand your expressive potential in preserving. You'll find examples in this book such as fresh thyme in grape jelly, cardamom with tart cherries, and Pernod with pears. Each of these seasonings contains essential oils that are aromatic and therefore volatile. Because of their ephemeral nature, herbs and spices need to be handled carefully.

I add herbs and liquors at the end of the cooking process. The herbs are not even "cooked" but are submerged and steeped in the finished preserve for a few minutes before it is ladled into jars. Distilled liquor is add at the very end of the

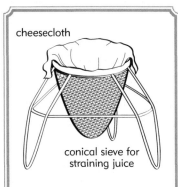

cheesecloth

conical sieve for straining juice

STRAINING JUICES

Select a clean tea towel or fine mesh cheesecloth to line a conical sieve or strainer to strain cooked fruit juices. If the cheesecloth is not a variety made specifically for kitchen use, wash it in mild soap to remove the sizing. Always dampen the cloth before pouring juices through it.

cooking process and boiled only a minute or two to drive off the alcohol. You can verify the strength of these additions by cooling a tablespoon of preserve quickly and tasting it. Add more seasoning and continue steeping or cooking if its presence is not discernable.

Spices, on the other hand, have sturdy oils that become embedded in the complex aroma of fruit preserves during cooking. I advise adding cinnamon stick, star anise, and ginger-root early in the cooking process. If there are a number of seasoning spices, tie them in cheesecloth so they will be easy to retrieve at the end of the cooking process.

FILLING JARS AND STORING PRESERVES

Pour the jelly, preserve, or marmalade into a large Pyrex measure once the jell is con-firmed. Jellies may need skimming to remove surface foam that will mar their clarity once poured into jars. Fruit preserves and mar-malades need to sit at least 5 minutes and be stirred occasionally to redistribute fruit pieces that will settle and become trapped in the jell as the mixture cools.

You may take this opportunity to transfer the sterilized jars from their hot water bath to the cooling rack. Briefly submerge the new lids and let them drain on a clean towel nearby. (The screw caps are not in contact with the seal and do not need special treat-ment.) You can also dip the plastic or metal funnel designed to fit inside the lip of the quilted jars.

Fit the funnel into the jars, one at a time, and pour in the preserve to within ¹⁄₄" of the lip.

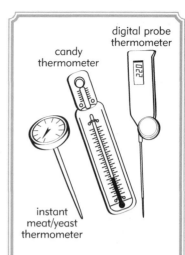

digital probe thermometer

candy thermometer

instant meat/yeast thermometer

THERMOMETERS

The digital probe thermometer with a 500-degree temperature range is now available for pre-serving. This is a pricey addition to one's supplies, but it's also an exact and instantaneous measuring device.

A candy thermometer fitted with a column of mercury is the time-honored guide to measuring the temperature in a pan of hot, bubbling preserves. Do not confuse a candy with a deep-fry thermometer: the candy thermometer defines temperature in two-degree increments while the one for deep-frying is calibrated every five degrees.

The instant meat/yeast thermometer has a range of 0° to 220°F., but I limit its use to testing baked goods.

15

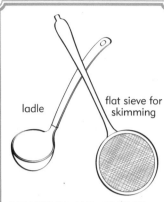

ladle

flat sieve for skimming

SKIMMING AND FILLING

A flat, fine-mesh stainless steel strainer makes easy work of skimming foam from jellies and jams. It also comes in handy as a means of removing telltale pips that rise to the surface of simmering marmalades. A large spoon with a shallow bowl is an alternative skimming device.

For the job of transferring hot preserves from the glass measure to the preserving jar, select a ladle with a half-cup bowl. Use a wide-mouth plastic funnel to fill hot jars without spilling.

funnel

8 oz. quilted jar

Thicker preserves with fruit pieces are better ladled into the jars to avoid splattering. Transfer the funnel to the next jar, and check the filled jar to make sure it is full enough and that no jelly has touched the edge of the lid. If this does occur, dip a paper towel in the recently boiling water and wipe the lip clean.

Attach the new lid and screw on the cap. Immediately invert the jar and hold it upside down for 10 seconds. This sterilizes the small layer of air that remained in the jar after filling. Return the jar to upright, and place it on the rack to cool. Proceed with the remaining jars.

A series of smart, cracking sounds emanating from the kitchen an hour or so after you finish working is proof that vacuum seals have formed on the finished preserves. Once they reach room temperature, place a colorful label on each jar for ease of identification. Don't delay this part of the job. You think you will remember what they are, but, take it from me, you won't be sure. A date is also a valuable addition to the label.

Store fruit preserves in a dark, cool spot. A cellar, basement storage area, or lower kitchen cabinet away from the heat are excellent for storage. But don't horde your jams and jellies! They will taste best if eaten within six months. Cooked preserves poured into unsterilized jars that are not vacuum sealed can be stored in the refrigerator or frozen.

Discard any preserve that develops mold, a fermented odor, or a changed appearance during storage. It was once common practice to simply scrape the mold off the top of jelly

Testing for Jell

Cold Plate Test:
Jelly will wrinkle on a cold plate if it has jelled.

Spoon Test:
Preserves will fall in a single sheet at 216° F.

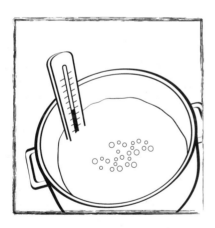

Thermometer Test:
Measure the temperature of water on your thermometer at boiling (212° F. at sea level).

Thermometer test:
Test for the jelling point by adding 8° to the temperature reading on your thermometer at boiling (220° F. at sea level).

and eat what lay beneath. We now know that these molds produce deep, invisible roots that carry mycotoxins that build up in the body over time. Be sure to refrigerate all preserves after opening. They are vulnerable to spoilage at room temperature once the vacuum seal is broken.

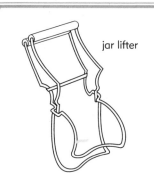
jar lifter

JAR LIFTER

This sturdy tool looks like a medieval torture device, but it actually protects the preserver from possible splashes of scalding water. No other device will lift jars as safely into a hot water bath from a cooling rack and back again. The jar lifter is available in hardware stores wherever canning supplies are sold.

HOT WATER BATH

Only the No-Sugar Jams in this book require a hot water bath after sealing, although you can process all preserves that way if you wish. The reason for this extra step is safety. The no-sugar preserves have no refined sugar to act as a preservative and are more vulnerable to spoilage.

This second cooking involves submerging the filled, sealed jars in boiling water and simmering them 10 minutes. There is a special lifting tool available wherever canning supplies are sold that makes transitions in and out of the bath quite easy. Once removed, jars should cool on a rack and be stored as described above.

PRESERVE EXPERIMENTS

As you gain experience in following recipes, your ability to experiment will emerge. Over time, you will become adept at efficiently timing and artfully balancing tastes, textures, and scents in preserves. The recipes in *Gourmet Preserves* are as precise as I can make them. But once you are comfortable with your own skills, let the experiments begin.

In addition to practice, I would also add patience to the list of qualities important to a preserving pro. A fruit preserve tastes different hot, when it has just been made, than it does when cooled. You will taste more sweet and sour flavors in warm, newly made preserves. These sensations overwhelm the aroma of the fruit and seasonings. Let your preserve cool and sit overnight before holding your critique. By that time the fruit essence and aroma will balance the flavors in the mouth.

WHAT TO DO WHEN THE JELLY WON'T JELL

From time to time, the desired jell does not occur as predicted, even when you think you've done everything correctly. You then have two choices. First you can change your expectations and decide that what you really wanted was a sauce for ice cream. You will certainly have something delicious to eat.

The second alternative is to apply a "pectin fix," using a small amount of commercial product. This formula will jell your preserves if they are thickened but syrupy:

- Pour the preserves into a glass measuring cup.
- For every cup of un-jelled preserves, measure out $1/2$ teaspoon Sure-Jell® powder and whisk in 2 tablespoons hot water. For example: 4 cups of preserve would require 2 teaspoons Sure-Jell and 8 tablespoons ($1/2$ cup) of hot water.
- Scrape this mixture into the preserves in a clean saucepan and return it to the boil.
- Stir in 1 teaspoon fresh lemon juice per cup of preserves.
- Bring the preserves to a boil and cook actively for 2–5 minutes.
- Pour the preserves out again into a clean glass measure.

FRESH VS. FROZEN FRUIT

The recipes in this book are designed for fresh fruits and berries. Dry-packed frozen fruits can be substituted in a pinch with this cautionary advice:

- Move fruits to the refrigerator to thaw completely before cooking them. Frozen fruits exude more juice when defrosted. They will need to cook longer to concentrate the juices.

- Frozen fruits may come more or less processed than fresh, sliced rather than whole, pitted rather than with pits. Make necessary translations in volume and weight to match the requirements of the recipe.
- The flavor of frozen fruit is not as vivid as fresh. To minimize this drawback, add a teaspoon more lemon juice per cup to accentuate the fruit flavor. You can strengthen the fruit's impact by greatly reducing its juices. Or you can go in another direction and combine the frozen fruit with a complementary fresh fruit.

DOUBLING AND TRIPLING RECIPES

Yes, these recipes can be doubled or tripled. If the result is more than 6 or 8 pounds of fruit, I prefer to work two batches side-by-side rather than risking a messy eruption from an overfilled pot. After spending a whole day picking peaches or berries, you may feel pressured to process your bounty quickly. But it will keep well for several days in the refrigerator, thereby allowing you time to work in small batches.

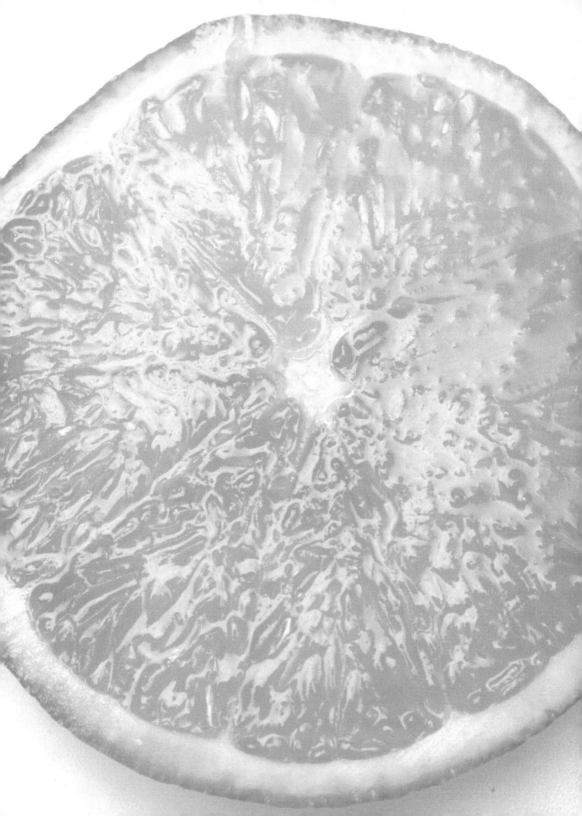

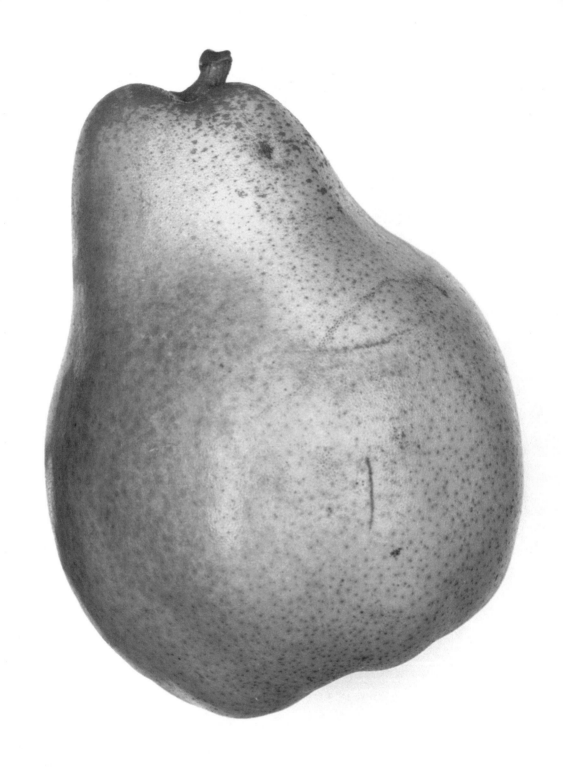

JAMS

Making fruit jam is the easiest technique for beginning preservers to master. Jams are simply cooked, sweetened fruit. You don't have to think about the jell. This gives you time to inhale the ripe scents of simmering fruit and enjoy your budding talent. Your success is guaranteed.

Despite its simplicity, my directions for making jams are specific. There is a rationale behind asking you to prepare these preserves with care. Attention to detail will add quality and a sense of craftsmanship to your jam. You'll be asked, for example, to cut pineapple into wedges in one recipe and pulverize it in another. Pears are diced in one recipe and thinly sliced in another. As each pound of fruit or berries cooks and reduces (to about 1 cup of pulp and concentrated juices), these initial shapes will affect the jam's texture. This will become the jam's mouth feel. As you gain experience in making preserves, you will learn to recognize the characteristic crunch of slender apple slices and the slippery feel of pine-apple strands on the tongue as physical sensations essential to the taste of jam. Anticipating these flavors and textures is one of the pleasures of preserving at home.

Another way to affect the consistency of jam is by limiting or extending the cooking time, depending on whether you prefer a looser or thicker jam. The amount of sugar added to the pan is also variable. The sweeter fruit ingredients may call for as little as $1/4$ cup of sugar per cup of reduced fruit.

Blueberries, for example, need minimal sweetening and cooking to offer their characteristic fragrance and soft texture. A tart fruit, such as rhubarb, by contrast, will require a cup or more of sugar to sweeten the same volume. I have tried to minimize the amount of sugar so that the fruit flavor dominates. You can vary this to suit your taste without compromising the recipe.

You may be surprised to find that jams made with high-pectin fruits such as blueberry, blackberry, and black raspberry will jell without your intending them to do so. Leaving them in this chapter is an arbitrary decision on my part. Other recipes titled Quick Preserves in Chapter 7 share the same technique but are intentionally designed to jell.

TECHNIQUE FOR MAKING JAMS
- Prepare the fruit for preserving.
- Measure the sugar, and reserve it.
- Begin cooking with the pot covered and the heat at medium. Once simmering, uncover and simmer as directed.
- Add sugar as directed.
- Cook for a specified time, until a temperature is reached, or until a desired thickness of texture is achieved.
- Vacuum seal the preserves as directed.

Strawberry Jam

Chamomile herbal tea adds the scent of new-mown hay to the bright sweetness of strawberries. It's an exhilarating taste treat to prepare in early spring.

YIELD: 3 CUPS

- 2 **pounds strawberries (8 cups quartered)**
- ¹/₂ **cup water**
- 2 **tablespoons lemon juice**
- 1 **cup sugar**
- 2 **bags chamomile tea (optional)**

Rinse, stem, and quarter the strawberries. Combine them with the water in a non-reactive 5-quart saucepan. Cover and bring to a boil. Uncover and simmer for 10 minutes, stirring occasionally to prevent sticking.

Stir in the lemon juice, and add the sugar ½ cup at a time, waiting for the liquid to return to the boil before adding more. Continue simmering another 5 minutes, stirring frequently. Cook only until the jam threatens to stick to the pot.

Pour the jam into a 1-quart measure. Submerge 2 bags of chamomile tea, if desired. Press the bags against the side of the container and steep for 10 minutes. Remove the bags.

Fill hot, sterilized jars to within ¼ inch of lips. Wipe the rims clean, attach new lids, and screw caps on tightly. Invert jars briefly to vacuum seal, or process in a boiling water bath, submerged by 1 inch, for 10 minutes.

Strawberry Rhubarb Jam

Although this classic combination is delicious on Risen Biscuits and English Muffins (see Index), you can turn it into the main event in a number of desserts. Fill a pre-baked tart shell with jam, and decorate it with fresh strawberry halves and a red currant glaze. If the weather is too hot for baking, freeze it, diluted with a simple syrup or light cream for a spectacular soft-frozen treat. The sensuous blend of silken rhubarb strands and soft berries is delicious at any temperature.

YIELD: 5 ½ CUPS

- **2 pounds strawberries**
- **1 pound rhubarb**
- **1 cup water**
- **10 strips lemon peel (approximately 3 inches long and ¼ inch wide)**
- **Juice of 1 lemon**
- **2 cups sugar**

Rinse and drain the berries. Remove the stems and hull them. Cut berries into a uniform size, and place in a heavy, non-reactive 8-quart pan. Add the rhubarb that has been rinsed, trimmed, and cut into ½-inch lengths. Add the lemon peel strips and water. Cover the pot and bring liquid to a boil. Simmer, uncovered, for 15 minutes.

Add lemon juice, then the sugar ½ cup at a time, waiting until liquids come to a simmer again before adding more. Continue to cook on medium heat for 10 minutes, stirring regularly to keep the mixture from sticking to the bottom of the pan. Jam will reach a temperature of 212° F. When the bubbles are thick and the jam spits when stirred, turn off the heat.

Skim off foam. Fill hot, sterilized jars to within ¼ inch of lips. Wipe the rims clean, attach new lids, and screw caps on tightly. Invert jars briefly to vacuum seal, or process in a boiling water bath, submerged by 1 inch, for 10 minutes.

Rhubarb Fig Jam

Bits of dried figs remain intact in this jam and leave nuggets of pure sweetness scattered throughout the tangy rhubarb strands. This bold texture is the key to the exciting play of sweet, sour, and astringent sensations on the palate.

Prolong this eating pleasure by spreading this jam on English Muffins (see Index), or tone it down with a muffin of contrasting texture such as Grape-Nuts® Muffins or Banana Bran Muffins (see Index).

YIELD: 5 CUPS

   2 pounds rhubarb stalks

   12 ounces dried Calamata figs

   1 cup water

   1 tablespoon fresh lemon juice

   1 ¹/₂ cups sugar

Rinse, trim, and cut rhubarb into ¹/₂-inch pieces. Cut off tough tips of fig stems, and cut each fig into 8 bits. Place the figs on the bottom of a deep, non-reactive 5-quart pan, followed by the rhubarb. Pour in the water, cover, and bring liquid to a boil. Uncover and simmer for 10 minutes, stirring occasionally to prevent sticking.

Add lemon juice and then the sugar ¹/₂ cup at a time. Return to a boil for 10 minutes or until the jam is thick and holds its shape when cooled on a chilled plate.

Fill hot, sterilized jars to within ¹/₄ inch of lips. Wipe the rims clean, attach new lids, and screw caps on tightly. Invert jars briefly for a quick vacuum seal, or process in a boiling water bath, submerged by 1 inch, for 10 minutes.

27

Apple Ginger Jam

Not to be confused with applesauce, this soft preserve contains firm apple bits and chewy fragments of peel. The addition of tart lemon juice and tingling gingerroot slices guarantees a good balance of sweet, sour, and spicy sensations.

This jam would taste great on Apple Cinnamon Muffins or Buttermilk Currant Scones (see Index for recipes). You could easily use it to make an Apple Jam Tart garnished with fresh apple slices, or freeze it using the Philadelphia–Style Ice Cream recipe (see Index). Wouldn't creamy apple ginger ice cream served with a warm burnt caramel sauce make a wonderful dessert?

YIELD: 5 CUPS

> 1 **cup water**
>
> ¹/₂ **tablespoon fresh lemon juice**
>
> 2 **pounds apples (use half Granny Smith, half Macintosh)**
>
> 3 **slices fresh ginger (size of a quarter)**
>
> 2¹/₂ **cups sugar**
>
> **Zest of 1 lemon**

Combine water and lemon juice in a heavy, non-reactive 5-quart pot. Scrub and rinse the apples. Quarter, core, and dice the apples, leaving the skin attached. (Dice apple quarters, in two batches, in the food processor, using a pulsing action.) Immediately toss apple pieces into the acidulated water. Add the ginger slices, cover, and bring to a boil. Uncover and simmer for 10 to 15 minutes until most juice is reduced.

Begin adding the sugar ½ cup at a time, allowing the liquid to regain the boil before adding more. Stir in thin strips of lemon peel removed with a zester. Lower the heat as the jam thickens, and cook another 5 minutes.

Off the heat, remove the ginger slices. Spoon the apple jam into hot, sterilized jars to within ¼ inch of the lips. Wipe rims clean, attach new lids, and screw caps on tightly. Invert the jars briefly for a quick vacuum seal, or process in a boiling water bath, submerged by 1 inch of water, for 10 minutes.

Ginger Pear Jam

A supply of knobby, fresh gingerroot is an indispensable ingredient for a wide range of condiments. This seasoning generates a surge of warmth on the tongue and a spicy fragrance that enhances the delicate floral aroma and taste of pears and many other fruits. Here, as elsewhere, the lemon juice adds just enough acid to balance the flavor of other ingredients. Savor the pleasures of this taste-tingling jam on Risen Biscuits or warm Cream Scones (see Index).

YIELD: 3 CUPS

　3 **pounds Bartlett pears**

$^1/_2$ **cup water**

　1 **tablespoon fresh lemon juice**

　2 **slices fresh gingerroot (size of a quarter)**

　1 **cup sugar**

Peel, quarter, and core the pears. Coarsely chop them. Combine pears in a heavy, non-reactive 5-quart pan with water, lemon juice, and ginger slices. Cover and bring mixture to a boil. Uncover and simmer for 15 minutes, stirring occasionally.

Add sugar ½ cup at a time, allowing the liquid to regain the boil before adding more. Continue cooking, uncovered, for another 10 minutes, stirring more frequently, until the jam is thickened.

Remove the ginger slices and fill hot, sterilized jars to within ¼ inch of lips. Wipe rims clean, attach new lids, and screw caps on tightly. Invert jars briefly for a quick vacuum seal, or process in a boiling water bath, submerged by 1 inch, for 10 minutes.

Pear and Pineapple Jam

Pears and pineapples, so different in taste and texture, make a wonderfully harmonious preserve that blends their flavors but respects the consistency and scent of each. A plateful of Oatmeal Muffins or Drop Scones (see Index) would complement this jam well.

YIELD: 3 ½ CUPS

> 2 **pounds Bartlett pears**
> 1 **pound peeled and cored pineapple**
> ½ **cup water**
> 1 **tablespoon fresh lemon juice**
> 1 **cup sugar**
> **Zest from 1 lemon**

Peel, quarter, and core pears. Cut pears and pineapple into pieces the size of lima beans. (If you are using a food processor, cut each fruit separately with the steel blade, making rapid on-and-off motions.)

Combine fruits with water and lemon juice in a heavy, non-reactive 5-quart pan. Cover and bring to a boil. Uncover and simmer for 15 minutes, stirring occasionally.

Add sugar ½ cup at a time, allowing the liquid to regain the boil before adding more. Continue cooking for 10 minutes, stirring frequently to prevent sticking. An instant-reading thermometer will rise to 212–214° F. as the jam reduces to 3 ½ cups. Off heat, stir in the lemon zest removed with a zester (illustrated on page 13).

Fill hot, sterilized jars to within ¼ inch of lips. Wipe rims clean, attach new lids, and screw on the caps tightly. Invert briefly for a quick vacuum seal, or process in a boiling water bath, submerged by 1 inch, for 10 minutes.

Pear and Plum Jam

*Although they rarely appear together, pears and plums are quite compatible fruits.
This recipe offers a quick and easy way to preserve their summer-fresh flavors
and aromas for cold-weather breakfasts or tea served with English Muffins or
Grape-Nuts® Muffins (see Index).*

YIELD: 4 ½ CUPS

> **2 pounds Bartlett pears**
> **1½ pounds Italian plums**
> **⅓ cup water**
> **1 tablespoon fresh lemon juice**
> **1 cup sugar**

Peel, core, and quarter pears. Scrub and rinse the plums. Halve plums
and remove their pits. Chop fruits into ½-inch pieces. (If you are using a
food processor, process each fruit separately with pulsing action.) Combine
the fruit pieces with water in a heavy, non-reactive 5-quart pan. Cover and
bring to a boil. Uncover and simmer for 10 minutes, stirring occasionally.

Add lemon juice and sugar ½ cup at a time, allowing the liquid to regain
the boil before adding more. Continue cooking, stirring frequently, until
there is little standing liquid on top of the fruit pulp and bubbles heave
mightily with a noisy plopping sound.

Fill hot, sterilized jars to within ¼ inch of the lips. Wipe rims clean, attach
new lids, and screw the caps on tightly. Invert the jars briefly for a quick
vacuum seal, or process in a boiling water bath, submerged by 1 inch,
for 10 minutes.

Raspberry Pear Jam

Red raspberries and pears make a dynamic pair that taste wonderful served fresh or cooked, hot or cold. This jam is delicious spread on a warm English Muffin or Cream Scone (see Index).

YIELD: 4 CUPS

  1 pound Bartlett pears
1½ pounds red raspberries
  ⅓ cup water
  2 tablespoons lemon juice
  2 cups sugar

Peel, quarter, core, and dice the pears. Combine them with raspberries and water in a heavy, non-reactive 5-quart saucepan. Cover and bring to a boil. Uncover and simmer for 10 minutes.

Add lemon juice and sugar ½ cup at a time, allowing the liquid to regain the boil before adding more. Partly cover the pot to prevent spattering when necessary. Also stir frequently to prevent sticking. Total cooking time will be about 15 minutes or until a finished temperature reading of 212° F. is attained. Jam will reduce to 1 quart.

Off heat, pour jam into hot, sterilized jars to within ¼ inch of the lips. Wipe rims clean, attach new lids, and screw the caps on tightly. Invert the jars briefly for a quick vacuum seal, or process in a boiling water bath, submerged by 1 inch, for 10 minutes.

Cherry Red Raspberry Jam

The red raspberries in this jam accentuate the less assertive flavor of the cherries. I serve this jam on special occasions and give it as gifts to friends. It is terrific on Butter Pecan Muffins, Cream Scones, and English Muffins (see Index).

YIELD: 4 1/2 CUPS

2 pounds pitted sour cherries (4 cups)
1 pound red raspberries (1 1/2 pints)
2 tablespoons fresh lemon juice
2 1/2 cups sugar

Place the cherries in the bowl of a food processor or blender and pulse for 15 seconds to coarsely chop them. Combine cherries with raspberries in a heavy, non-reactive 8-quart pot, cover, and bring to a boil. Uncover and simmer for 15 minutes to reduce the juices, stirring regularly. The mixture will thicken but should not stick.

Stir in the lemon juice, and begin adding sugar 1/2 cup at a time, waiting for the liquid to return to the simmer before adding more. Continue to stir frequently. Let the jam cook 10 minutes more. It will noticeably thicken, and the temperature will reach 216–218° F.

Pour the jam into a heat-resistant glass quart measure. Stir twice over a 5 minute period. Fill hot, sterilized jars to within 1/4 inch of lips. Wipe the rims clean, attach new lids, and screw caps on tightly. Invert the jars briefly for a quick vacuum seal, or process in a boiling water bath, submerged by 1 inch, for 10 minutes.

Cherry Vanilla Jam

YIELD: 4 CUPS

2 pounds pitted sour cherries (4 cups)

1 pound Granny Smith apples (2 $^1/_2$ cups peeled and chopped)

1 vanilla bean *or* 1 tablespoon vanilla extract

2 tablespoons fresh lemon juice

2 $^1/_4$ cups sugar

Place the cherries in the bowl of a food processor or blender and pulse for 15 seconds to chop them medium-fine. Peel, core, and quarter the apples. Chop them to a medium-fine texture in the food processor or blender, using a pulsing action. Combine the cherry and apple pieces in a heavy, non-reactive 5-quart pan.

Cut through the skin of the vanilla pod along its length. Use a paring knife to scrape the contents of the pod onto the knife. Add the vanilla pod and scraped beans to the fruit. Cover the pan and bring to a boil. Uncover and simmer for 15 minutes to reduce the juices, stirring regularly. The mixture will thicken but should not stick.

Stir in the lemon juice, then add sugar in four equal batches, waiting for the liquid to return to the simmer before adding more. Continue to stir frequently. Let the jam cook actively 10 minutes more. It will noticeably thicken and reach a temperature of 210–212° F.

Pour the jam into a heat-resistant 1-quart measure. Remove the vanilla pod. Fill hot, sterilized jars to within ¼ inch of lips. Wipe the rims clean, attach new lids, and screw caps on tightly. Invert the jars briefly for a quick vacuum seal, or process in a boiling water bath, submerged by 1 inch, for 10 minutes.

Red and Black Raspberry Jam with Cherries

YIELD: 5 CUPS

1 **pound black raspberries ($1^1/_2$ pints)**

1 **pound red raspberries ($1^1/_2$ pints)**

1 **pound sour cherries, pitted (2 cups)**

$^1/_2$ **cup water**

2 **tablespoons lemon juice**

$2^3/_4$ **cups sugar**

Combine cherries with raspberries and water in a heavy, non-reactive 5-quart pan, cover, and bring to a boil. Uncover and simmer for 15 minutes to reduce the juices, stirring regularly. The mixture will thicken but should not stick.

Add the lemon juice, then begin adding sugar in five equal batches, waiting for the liquid to return to the simmer before adding more. Continue to stir frequently. Let the jam cook 10 minutes more. It will noticeably thicken and the candy thermometer will read 216° F.

Off heat, fill hot, sterilized jars to within 1/4 inch of lips. Wipe the rims clean, attach new lids, and screw caps on tightly. Invert the jars briefly for a quick vacuum seal, or process in a boiling water bath, submerged by 1 inch, for 10 minutes.

Black Raspberry Cassis Jam

YIELD: 3 CUPS

2 pints black raspberries

2 pints black currants

$^1/_2$ cup water

2 tablespoons lemon juice

3 cups sugar

Rinse and combine the raspberries and currants. Place fruit in a non-reactive 5-quart saucepan. Pour in water, cover the pan, and bring to a boil. Uncover and simmer 15 minutes.

Remove seeds and skins by passing berries through the finest disk of a food mill. If the combined pulp and juice is less than 3 cups, add water to measure that amount. If the puree is more than 3 cups, increase amount of sugar called for to equal the same volume as the fruit.

Return mixture and lemon juice to a clean pan, and bring to a simmer, stirring frequently to prevent the pulp from sticking to the bottom. Add the sugar $^1/_2$ cup at a time, waiting for the jam to return to the simmer before adding more. Stir the pot after each addition to prevent the pulp from sticking.

Cook the jam at medium-high heat, stirring frequently, for 5 minutes longer. The thermometer will reach 216–218° F., and the jam will be very thick. This jam will coat the spoon generously .

Off heat, transfer the preserves to a 1-quart measure. Fill hot, sterilized jars to within ¼ inch of lips. Wipe rims clean, attach new lids, and screw caps on tightly. Either invert each jar briefly for a quick vacuum seal, or process in a boiling water bath, submerged by 1 inch, for 10 minutes.

Seedless Black Raspberry Jam

The concentrated essence of wild black raspberries in this jam recalls the cool, damp air trapped in wooded raspberry thickets on hot afternoons in early July.

YIELD: 3 CUPS

4 **pints black raspberries (2$\frac{1}{2}$ pounds)**

$\frac{1}{2}$ **cup water**

2 **tablespoons fresh lemon juice**

3$\frac{1}{2}$ **cups sugar**

Rinse berries and combine with water in a in a heavy, non-reactive 5-quart pan. Cover and bring to a simmer. Simmer, partially covered, for 10 minutes. Use a food mill fitted with the disk with the smallest openings to separate the juices and pulp from the seeds. The result will measure 3$\frac{1}{2}$ cups. If there is less, add water to measure that amount. If there is more, increase sugar called for to equal the same volume as the fruit pulp.

Pour the black raspberry pulp and the lemon juice into a clean 5-quart pan. Return to the simmer, and begin adding sugar $\frac{1}{2}$ cup at a time, allowing the juices to return to the simmer before adding more. Stir the pan each time you add sugar to prevent the pulp from sticking to the bottom. Cook over medium-high heat, now stirring every minute, until jam reaches 216–218° F. This should happen in 5 to 7 minutes. The preserves will be quite thick.

Fill hot, sterilized jars to within $\frac{1}{4}$ inch of the lips. Wipe the rims clean, attach new lids, and screw caps on tightly. Vacuum seal by briefly inverting the jars, or process in a boiling water bath, submerged by 1 inch, for 10 minutes.

Rhubarb Ginger Jam

Rhubarb jam with ginger was one of the first fruit preserves I ever made. I was thrilled with its dramatic balance of tart rhubarb, hot ginger, and sweet sugar.

I recommend you first try this jam on chewy English Muffins (see Index) so you can fully enjoy the taste and texture of clusters of rhubarb strands and exciting hot tiny bits of crystallized ginger.

YIELD: 3 CUPS

    2 pounds fresh rhubarb
    8 3-inch strips lemon peel (approximately ¼ inch wide)
    2 fresh gingerroot slices (size of a quarter)
    ½ cup water
    1 tablespoon lemon juice
    2½ cups sugar
    2 ounces (⅓ cup) thinly sliced crystallized ginger

Rinse, trim, and cut fresh rhubarb stalks into ½-inch lengths. Combine with lemon strips (removed with a stripper, illustrated on page 13), gingerroot slices, and water in a heavy, non-reactive 5-quart pan. Cover and bring to a boil. Uncover and simmer for 10 minutes, stirring occasionally.

Add lemon juice and sugar ½ cup at a time, waiting for the liquid to return to the boil before adding more. Continue cooking over high heat, stirring constantly, until the jam thickens and bubble pattern becomes quite dense. Stir in the crystallized ginger pieces at the end of the cooking period.

Off heat, remove the gingerroot. Fill hot, sterilized jars to within ¼ inch of lips. Wipe rims clean, attach new lids, and screw caps on tightly. Invert jars briefly for a quick vacuum seal, or process in a boiling water bath, submerged by 1 inch, for 10 minutes.

Rhubarb Blackberry Jam

Since fresh rhubarb and blackberries are not always available at the market at the same time, you will have to supply your own from the garden or substitute a frozen product for one of the fruits. Let the frozen fruit come almost to room temperature before starting the recipe. The frozen fruit will exude more liquid than the fresh and may require a slightly longer cooking time. Serve this jam with any one of the chewy English Muffin recipes (see Index).

YIELD: 3 CUPS

$^3/_4$ **pound rhubarb**

1 **pound fresh blackberries**

$^1/_2$ **cup water**

1 **tablespoon lemon juice**

1 $^3/_4$ **cups sugar**

Rinse and trim rhubarb. Cut it into $^1/_2$-inch lengths. Combine rhubarb and blackberries with water in a heavy, non-reactive 5-quart pan. Cover and bring to a boil. Uncover and simmer for 10 minutes until the fruits soften and release juice but remain whole.

Add lemon juice, then sugar in three equal batches, returning the liquid to the boil after each addition. Stir jam continuously until it thickens noticeably and the bubble pattern is quite dense. Temperature of jam should be 210° F.

Fill hot, sterilized jars to within $^1/_4$ inch of lips. Wipe off rims, attach new lids, and screw caps on tightly. Invert briefly for a quick vacuum seal, or process in a boiling water bath, submerged by 1 inch, for 10 minutes.

Apricot Blueberry Jam

The cooking time for this jam is short, and little sugar is added, so the generous yield of soft, reduced fruit pieces is intensely fresh tasting. This jam is delicious served with Zucchini Bread or Grape-Nuts® Muffins (see Index).

YIELD: 5 ½ CUPS

2 pounds apricots (4 cups after peeling and pitting)

½ cup water

1 pound blueberries

2 tablespoons lemon juice

1 cup sugar

Dip the apricots in boiling water for 30 seconds. Move them to an iced water bath. When cool enough to handle, slip off their skins, remove pits, and slice apricots. Combine apricots with water in a heavy, non-reactive 5-quart saucepan. Cover and bring to a boil. Uncover and simmer, stirring frequently, for 5 minutes.

Rinse the blueberries, and stir into the apricot mixture. Cover and bring the jam back to the simmer. Uncover and cook for 10 minutes.

Add lemon juice, then sugar ½ cup at a time, waiting for the liquid to return to the boil before adding more. Continue cooking over high heat, stirring constantly, until the jam thickens and bubble pattern becomes quite dense. The jam should pass the cold plate test.

Pour the jam into hot, sterilized jars to within ¼ inch of the lips. Wipe the rims clean, attach new lids, and screw the caps on tightly. Invert the jars briefly for a quick vacuum seal, or process in a boiling water bath, submerged by 1 inch, for 10 minutes.

Apricot Orange Jam

The acidic bite of orange juice and its fresh citrus scent accentuate the perfumed sweetness of the apricots. Together they make a sunny, light preserve that is perfect for a brunch buffet, spread on freshly baked Risen Biscuits or Cornmeal Muffins (see Index).

YIELD: 3 CUPS

2 pounds ripe apricots, skins removed, pitted, and thinly sliced (4 cups)

1 6-ounce can unsweetened orange juice concentrate

$^3/_4$ cup water

1$^1/_4$ cups sugar

Zest of 1 orange

$^1/_4$ cup apricot liqueur

Dip the apricots in boiling water for 30 seconds. Move them to an iced water bath. When cool enough to handle, slip off their skins, remove pits, and slice apricots. Combine the slices with orange juice concentrate and water in a heavy, non-reactive 5-quart pan. Cover and bring to a boil. Uncover and simmer for 10 minutes, stirring regularly. Apricot slices will cook and soften. As the mixture thickens, bubbles will become small and tightly packed. Portions of it will begin to heave and plop.

Add the sugar in three equal batches, waiting for the liquid to return to a boil before adding more. Continue to stir and simmer on low for 10 minutes. Add orange zest and liqueur, and cook another 2 minutes to thicken jam a bit more. Stir continuously at this point to prevent sticking.

Fill hot, sterilized jars to within $^1/_4$ inch of lips. Wipe the rims clean, attach new lids, and screw caps on tightly. Vacuum seal by inverting briefly, or process in a boiling water bath, submerged by 1 inch, for 10 minutes.

Peach Blueberry Jam

A jam made with sliced peaches and blueberries retains fresh and delicate fruit flavors when it is cooked briefly and gently. Enjoy the subtlety of this jam with Cream Scones, Risen Biscuits, or Oatmeal Muffins (see Index).

YIELD: 3 ½ CUPS

    2 pounds peaches (3 cups)

½ cup water

    1 pound blueberries

    2 tablespoons lemon juice

    3 cups sugar

Dip the peaches in boiling water for 30 seconds. Move to an iced water bath. When cool enough to handle, peel off the skins, pit, and thinly slice. Combine peach slices with water in a deep, non-reactive 5-quart saucepan. Cover and bring to a boil. Uncover and simmer, stirring frequently, for 10 minutes. Peaches will become thick with bubbles. The pot will make a hissing sound as you pull the spoon across the bottom, but the peach pulp will not stick.

Stir in the blueberries, cover the pan, and return the mixture to a boil. Uncover and simmer for 10 minutes. Add lemon juice, then sugar ½ cup at a time, waiting for the liquid to return to a boil before adding more. Simmer for 5 minutes or until thickened. A thermometer reading at this point should be 210° F.

Fill hot, sterilized jars to within ¼ inch of lips. Wipe the rims clean, attach new lids, and screw caps on tightly. Invert jars briefly for a quick vacuum seal, or process jars in a boiling water bath, submerged by 1 inch, for 10 minutes.

Kiwifruit Pineapple Jam

Kiwifruit is a newcomer to preserving. Originally a native of New Zealand, kiwifruit is now grown in California and available throughout the year at reasonable prices. Its acid-green color and tiny black seeds are quite dramatic but fade as you cook it.

The pineapple and kiwifruit have similar flavor profiles. They are lusciously sweet when ripe but acidic to the point of astringency before that. The sugar you add will temper the fruit acid and allow their distinct and complementary tastes to mingle.

YIELD: 3 ½ CUPS

> 6 **large kiwifruits (3 cups)**
> 1½ **pounds peeled and cored pineapple (4 cups)**
> ½ **cup water**
> 2 **tablespoons lemon juice**
> 3 **cups sugar**

Peel and quarter kiwifruits lengthwise. Slice quarters into thin pie-shaped wedges. (If using a food processor, chop 3 kiwifruits at a time, quartered, with rapid on and off motions, until they are ½-inch bits.)

Chop the pineapple into ¼-inch wedges, or chop with rapid pulsing in the food processor.

Combine the pineapple, kiwifruit pieces, and water in a heavy, non-reactive 5-quart pan. Cover and bring to a boil. Uncover and simmer for 10 minutes.

Add lemon juice, then sugar ½ cup at a time, waiting for the liquid to return to a boil before adding more. Continue to boil for 10 more minutes or until the jam reaches 216° F.

Off heat, skim foam from the surface.

Fill hot, sterilized jars to within ¼ inch of lips. Wipe the rims clean, attach new lids, and screw caps on tightly. Invert jars briefly for a vacuum seal, or process in a boiling water bath, submerged by 1 inch, for 10 minutes.

Kiwifruit Mint Jam

A touch of citrus fragrance and the cool, soothing sensation of fresh mint in this kiwifruit jam highlight the considerable flavor range of this fuzzy little fruit. It is sweet, a bit acidic (particularly before it ripens), and its scent recalls ripe bananas and strawberries. Savor the subtlety of this jam spread on English Muffins or a Cream Scone (see Index).

YIELD: 2⅔ CUPS

- **2 pounds ripe kiwifruit**
- **⅓ cup water**
- **2 tablespoons lemon juice**
- **2 cups sugar**
- **Zest of 1 lemon**
- **3 6-inch sprigs fresh mint**

Peel and quarter kiwifruit. Slice thinly and combine with water in a heavy, non-reactive 5-quart pan. Cover and bring to a boil. Uncover and simmer for 10 minutes, stirring every 2 to 3 minutes.

Add lemon juice, then sugar ½ cup at a time, waiting for the liquid to return to a boil before adding more. Continue cooking briskly and stirring until jam mixture thickens and there is a tight pattern of bubbles over the top. This will happen in less than 5 minutes. The temperature of the hot liquid should be 212° F.

Off heat, pour the jam into a 1-quart measure. Stir in the lemon zest and mint sprigs. Crush the mint stems along the bottom and sides of the container. Let mint steep for 5 minutes. Cool a spoonful of jam and taste. Remove the stems when the taste of mint is noticeable but before it is pronounced.

Fill hot, sterilized jars to within ¼ inch of lips. Wipe the rims clean, attach new lids, and screw caps on tightly. Invert jars briefly for a quick vacuum seal, or process in a boiling water bath, submerged by 1 inch, for 10 minutes.

Nectarine Jam with Grand Marnier

The nectarine is a variety of peach with a fine flavor and good acidity. Try it with Grape-Nuts® Muffins or Butter Pecan Muffins (see Index).

YIELD: 3 ½ CUPS

3 pounds ripe nectarines (5 ½ cups)

⅓ cup water

1 cup sugar

¼ cup Grand Marnier liqueur

2 tablespoons fresh lemon juice

Submerge the nectarines for 30 seconds in boiling water. Cool them immediately in a bowl of iced water. Peel them when cool enough to handle. Cut the meat away from the stone and chop into small pieces. You will have about 5 ½ cups of fruit.

Combine nectarine pieces with water in a heavy, non-reactive 5-quart saucepan. Cover and bring to a boil. Uncover and simmer for 10 minutes, stirring occasionally to prevent sticking.

Stir in the sugar ½ cup at a time, returning liquid to a simmer before adding more. Allow liquids to reduce over medium heat, stirring frequently. This will take about 15 minutes. When the jam thickens noticeably, stir, and pour in the Grand Marnier and lemon juice. Reduce quickly, stirring constantly for another 2 minutes.

Fill hot, sterilized jars to within ¼ inch of lips. Wipe the rims clean, attach new lids, and screw caps on tightly. Invert jars briefly for a quick vacuum seal, or process in a boiling water bath, submerged by 1 inch, for 10 minutes.

Pineapple Blueberry Jam

A jam of pineapple and blueberries is bound to contain rich contrasts in taste, texture, and scent. A fresh, warm plateful of English Muffins (see Index) and cold sweet butter are definitely in order for sampling it.

YIELD: 3 CUPS

1^1/$_4$ pounds peeled and cored pineapple

^{1}/$_3$ cup water

1^1/$_2$ tablespoons fresh lime juice

1^1/$_2$ cups sugar, divided

1 pound fresh blueberries

Chop the pineapple into ^{1}/$_4$-inch wedges, or chop with rapid pulsing in the food processor. Combine pineapple pieces and water in a heavy, non-reactive 5-quart saucepan. Cover and bring to a boil. Uncover and simmer for 15 minutes or until almost all juice is reduced.

Stir in the lime juice, then add ^{1}/$_2$ cup sugar. Boil, uncovered, for 10 minutes, stirring frequently. Stop cooking if fruit pieces threaten to stick to the bottom.

Stir in the blueberries, cover the pan, and return jam to a simmer. Uncover and cook 10 minutes, stirring regularly. Add the remaining cup of sugar, ^{1}/$_2$ cup at a time. Cook the jam over medium-high heat for another 5 minutes, stirring every minute or so. Jam is ready when liquids pass the spoon test, that is, when a metal spoonful of jam is tipped, the liquid should fall in a single sheet rather than in separate drops (illustrated on page 17). A thermometer should register 210° F.

Fill hot, sterilized jars to within ^{1}/$_4$ inch of the lips. Wipe rims clean, attach new lids, and screw caps on tightly. Invert jars briefly for a quick vacuum seal, or process in a boiling water bath, submerged by 1 inch, for 10 minutes.

Tomato Prune Jam

This recipe is for the more adventuresome eater who seeks out new taste experiences. Tomatoes and prunes make quite a mild, sweet blend; the red wine vinegar added at the very end contrasts and accentuates the ingredients. This soft, spreadable jam is great on warm Oatmeal Muffins and Buttermilk Currant Scones (see Index).

YIELD: 4 CUPS

- 12 ounces pitted prunes
- 2 pounds ripe tomatoes (4–5 medium)
- Bouquet garni: 1 cinnamon stick, 3 cloves, 3 allspice berries, 2 lemon peel strips
- 2 tablespoons lemon juice
- 1/2 cup granulated sugar
- 1/2 cup brown sugar
- 1 tablespoon (or more to taste) red wine vinegar

Cut prunes into 1/2-inch pieces. Dip the tomatoes in simmering water for 30 seconds. Cool in an iced water bath. When cool enough to handle, slip off the skins, core, and quarter the tomatoes. Force out seeds into a fine strainer and reserve the juices. Coarsely chop tomato pieces.

Combine prunes, tomatoes, strained juices, and bouquet garni in a deep, non-reactive 4-quart saucepan. Cover and bring to a simmer. Uncover and simmer for 15 minutes, stirring regularly. (The mixture will thicken and be free of standing liquid.)

Stir in the lemon juice, then the sugars one at a time. Continue cooking for another 10 minutes until the jam is thick again and a thermometer reads 208–210° F.

Off heat, remove the bouquet, and stir in the vinegar. Quickly cool a tablespoon of jam in the freezer and taste for the slightly tart finish of the vinegar to balance the sweet fruits. Add more vinegar if desired.

Fill hot, sterilized jars to within $\frac{1}{4}$ inch of the lips. Wipe the rims clean, attach new lids, and screw caps on tightly. Process in a boiling water bath, submerged by 1 inch, for 10 minutes. Alternatively, quick-seal by inverting the jars briefly.

Tomato Basil Jam

I could not resist the desire to bring the synergetic team of tomato and basil into this collection. Balance is important here. You will want to cool and taste this jam carefully to bring sweet and sour elements into equilibrium. Add the remaining basil strips as the jam cools so they retain their vivid green color. This jam is quite good with Risen Biscuits and Whole-Wheat English Muffins (see Index).

YIELD: 2½–3 CUPS

3 **pounds ripe tomatoes**

2 **lemons**

24 **fresh basil leaves, divided**

1 **cup sugar**

Dip the tomatoes in simmering water for 30 seconds. Cool them in an iced water bath. When cool enough to handle, peel, core, quarter, and squeeze seeds out though a sieve to retain juices. Coarsely chop the tomatoes. Pieces and reserved juice will measure a generous 4 cups.

Place tomatoes in a deep, non-reactive 4-quart pan. Cover and bring to a boil. Uncover and simmer for 30 minutes or until the jam is reduced to 2½ to 3 cups and free of excess moisture.

While the tomatoes simmer, remove the yellow zest from the 2 lemons with a zester (illustrated on page 13). Squeeze the juice from both lemons. Puree 12 basil leaves with ½ of the lemon juice.

Off heat, stir the zest and the lemon juice without the basil into the tomatoes. Return the tomato mixture to a simmer, and begin adding the sugar ½ cup at a time, allowing the mixture to regain the boil before adding more. Cook and stir frequently for 10 minutes, until the jam thickens again. The thermometer reading should be 210° F.

Off heat, stir in remaining lemon-basil juice. Cool a tablespoon of jam briefly. When cooled to room temperature, taste for a balance of sweet and sour.

Add more lemon juice by the tablespoon as needed. Cut the remaining basil leaves into thin strips. Fold them into the jam.

Fill hot, sterilized jars to within $\frac{1}{4}$ inch of the lips. Wipe rims clean, attach new lids, and screw caps on tightly. Invert the jars briefly to force out the air for a quick seal, or process them in a boiling water bath, submerged by 1 inch, for 10 minutes.

Tomato Orange Jam

This jam celebrates my favorite winter lunch drink, a mug of hot V-8®juice flavored with a little orange juice and scented with spices. It's a taste combination that works beautifully in a preserve with fresh tomatoes. You can warm the jam if you like by heating it in the oven. Try it on fresh Cornmeal Muffins (see Index).

YIELD: ALMOST 3 CUPS

3 pounds ripe tomatoes

2 navel oranges

Bouquet garni: 3 cloves, 3 allspice berries, 1 slice fresh ginger

1 cup sugar

2 tablespoons unsweetened orange juice concentrate (optional)

Tomato paste (optional)

Submerge tomatoes in boiling water for 30 seconds. Move to an iced water bath. When cool enough to handle, peel, core, and quarter. Force out seeds and liquid through a sieve; coarsely chop the pulp. Tomato pieces and strained juices will measure about 4 cups.

Remove the zest from both oranges with a zester (illustrated on page 13). Cut away and discard inner white peel. Halve the oranges, remove seeds, and thinly slice.

Combine tomatoes with juices, orange zest, orange slices, and the bouquet garni in a deep, non-reactive 4-quart saucepan. Cover and bring to a boil. Uncover and simmer for 25 minutes or until the mixture has reduced to 3 cups.

Stir in sugar ½ cup at a time, allowing the jam to return to the simmer between additions. Cook at a simmer for another 10 minutes until reduced again to about 3 cups. Temperature of mixture will reach 210° F.

Off heat, remove bouquet garni. Cool a tablespoon of jam in the freezer and taste for an even blend of tomato and orange flavors. Add orange juice concentrate or a little tomato paste as needed for balance.

Fill hot, sterilized jars to within $1/4$ inch of the lips. Wipe rims clean, attach new lids, and screw caps on tightly. Invert jars briefly to quick-seal, or process in a boiling water bath, submerged by 1 inch, for 10 minutes.

Green Tomato Jam

You may be surprised to find that unripe tomatoes cook into a mild, sweet jam. The lemon, apple, and cinnamon add greater subtlety. Cornmeal Muffins and Buttermilk Currant Scones (see Index) offer interesting taste and texture contrasts.

YIELD: 3 ½ CUPS

2 pounds green tomatoes

2 lemons

1 tart apple

¹/₂ cup water

1 4-inch cinnamon stick

1 cup sugar

Scrub and rinse all of the fruits. Remove the stem ends of the tomatoes and dice them by hand or chop them two at a time, quartered, in a food processor fitted with a steel blade, using rapid pulsing action. Remove the zest from the lemons with a zester (illustrated on page 13). Cut off and discard the inner white peel. Halve the lemons and thinly slice, removing seeds. Peel, quarter, core, and dice the apple.

Combine the tomatoes, lemon zest, lemon slices, and apple pieces with the water and cinnamon stick in a heavy, non-reactive 4-quart pan. Cover the pan and bring liquid to a boil. Uncover and simmer for 15 minutes.

Add sugar ½ cup at a time, allowing the jam to return to the simmer between additions. Cook, uncovered, for 10 minutes, stirring frequently. The temperature will rise to 210° F.

Off heat, remove the cinnamon stick. Pour the jam into hot, sterilized jars to within ¼ inch of lips. Wipe rims clean, attach new lids, and screw the caps on tightly. Invert the jars briefly for a quick vacuum seal, or process for 10 minutes in a boiling water bath, submerged by 1 inch.

Spicy Cranberry Jam

Why should the cranberry be relegated to salad molds when it makes such a zesty preserve? This jam recipe is quite easy to prepare, and it makes a terrific topping with all holiday breads. Warm Butter Pecan Muffins or Whole Wheat English Muffins (see Index) are my bread choices from this book.

You could easily freeze this cranberry jam, using my sorbet formula (see Index), and serve it as a festive and colorful palate freshener at the beginning or end of a rich winter meal.

YIELD: 6 CUPS

2 pounds cranberries

$^1/_2$ cup water

Bouquet garni: 1 4-inch cinnamon stick, $^1/_2$ teaspoon fennel seed, 2 whole cloves, 3 allspice berries, 1 slice ginger

4 cups sugar

Pick over and remove bruised cranberries before weighing them. Rinse them and combine with water in a heavy, non-reactive 4-quart pan. Cover the pan, and bring berries to a boil. Submerge bouquet garni in the cranberry mixture. Uncover and simmer for 10 minutes.

Stir in the sugar, $^1/_2$ cup at a time, allowing the jam to return to the boil before adding more. Partly cover the pot if jam begins to spit. Continue to cook until the jam thickens and temperature rises to 214° F., but no more than 20 minutes.

Off heat, let the spices steep an additional 5 minutes before removing them. Pour the jam into hot, sterilized jars to within $^1/_4$ inch of the lips. Wipe the rims clean, attach new lids, and screw the caps on tightly. Invert the jars briefly for a quick vacuum seal, or process in a boiling water bath, submerged by 1 inch, for 10 minutes.

Damson Plum Jam

Since these petite plums, the color of eggplant, ripen quickly and are not widely grown, you may have to look hard to find them at the market. They are intensely sour when fresh, but when cooked, their preserved essence of plum develops into a superb sweet-sour flavor.

This jam is crimson and spicy-sweet if cooked only to 214° F. As you continue to cook it to 218° F., it becomes darker, firmer, and more tart. Pair this assertive jam with vigorous breads such as Buckwheat Muffins or Tea Brack (see Index).

YIELD: ABOUT 6 CUPS

4 pounds Damson plums

1 cup water

Sugar

Scrub, rinse, and stem plums. Combine plums and water in a heavy, non-reactive 8-quart pan. Cover and bring to a boil. Uncover and simmer for 30 minutes.

Let the cooked plums cool briefly, then pass them through a sieve or food mill to separate the pits and skins from the pulp. Measure the plum pulp, and set aside 1 cup sugar for every full cup of plum puree.

Place plum pulp in a clean 8-quart pan, cover, and heat slowly to a boil. Begin adding sugar about ½ cup at a time, allowing the jam to return to a boil between additions. After all the sugar is added, insert a candy thermometer and continue cooking, stirring frequently, until the temperature reaches 214° F.

Off heat, give the jam the cold plate test. (Pour a teaspoon of hot jam onto a chilled plate and refrigerate it for 1 minute. The jam sample will cool to its finished consistency.) If you like the consistency, stop the cooking now. For a firmer jelled jam, cook the jam another 5 minutes or to a temperature reading of up to 218° F. Stir almost constantly the last few minutes.

Off heat, skim the jam and pour it into hot, sterilized jars to within ¼ inch of the lips. Wipe off the rims, attach new lids, and screw caps on tightly. Invert the jars briefly for a quick vacuum seal, or process in a boiling water bath, submerged by 1 inch, for 10 minutes.

Plum Jam with Cardamom

Plum skins have a pleasant acidic tang that invite the heady fragrance of cardamom seeds. This assertive jam tastes best with an equally vigorous bread like Buckwheat Muffins or Whole-Wheat English Muffins (see Index).

YIELD: 3 CUPS

2 pounds Italian plums (3 $^1/_3$ cups)

5 cardamom pods

$^1/_3$ cup water

1 cup sugar

Scrub, rinse, and wipe off the plums. Halve them, remove pits, and finely chop. (If you are using a food processor, cut the plums with rapid pulsing action.) Tie cardamom pods in a piece of cheesecloth with cotton twine and crush them lightly with a rolling pin. Combine them with the plums and water in a heavy, non-reactive 4-quart pan. Cover and bring to a boil. Uncover and simmer for 10 minutes.

Begin adding sugar $^1/_2$ cup at a time, waiting for the mixture to regain the boil before adding more. Continue to cook, stirring regularly to prevent sticking, until the mixture is quite thick.

Off heat, remove cardamom seeds. Fill hot, sterilized jars to within $^1/_4$ inch of the lips. Wipe rims clean, attach new lids, and screw caps on tightly. Invert jars briefly for a quick vacuum seal, or process in a boiling water bath, submerged by 1 inch, for 10 minutes.

Quince Jam

A ripe quince has such a rich apple perfume that you may hesitate to cook yours, preferring instead to cluster a few in a bowl to place where their fragrance can be appreciated. Once you begin to prepare this fruit for cooking and see how hard and woody it is to cut, how positively astringent it is in the mouth, you will be convinced that the market sold you the wrong fruit. Don't give up. Cooking and sweetening will thoroughly subdue and transform the quince into a soft and mild jam with a lovely apple scent. Enjoy the delicacy of Quince Jam on Oatmeal Muffins or Drop Scones (see Index).

YIELD: 6 CUPS

1 **quart water**

2 **tablespoons fresh lemon juice, divided**

3 **pounds quinces**

1^1/$_2$ **cups sugar**

Combine water with 1 tablespoon of lemon juice in a heavy, non-reactive 5-quart pan.

Peel, quarter, and core the quinces. Cut the quarters into eighths or smaller uniform pieces. As soon as each quince is cut, stir it into the acidulated water. This will keep them from discoloring.

Cover the pan, and bring liquid to a boil. Uncover and simmer for 30 minutes. Remove about half of the tender quince pieces from the pan. Cut these into small dice. Puree the remaining quince pieces with the liquid.

Return the quince pieces and the puree to a clean 5-quart saucepan. Cover and return to a boil. Uncover, add the remaining tablespoon of lemon juice, and begin adding the sugar ^{1}/$_2$ cup at a time, allowing the mixture to return to a boil before adding more. The jam will be quite thick and will require frequent stirring to prevent sticking. Cook until the jam will hold its shape on a spoon for no more than 5 minutes.

Off heat, ladle the jam into hot, sterilized jars to within $\frac{1}{4}$ inch of the lips. Wipe rims clean, attach new lids, and screw caps on tightly. Invert the jars briefly for a quick vacuum seal, or process for 10 minutes in a boiling water bath, submerged by 1 inch.

Blueberry Jam with Mint

This recipe is technically a hybrid, mixing two steps from the preserve technique with the jam process. The sugar is added cup for cup with the fruit, and it is cooked to the jell point. However, the berries are never strained, steeped, or reduced but remain whole in the pot during the entire cooking process, which is typical of jam making. The result is a larger than usual yield of a sweet, delicate jam that is lightly jelled.

Try this jam with Butter Pecan Muffins, or pour it over hot French Toast, Buckwheat Blinis, or the Giant Sunday Popover (see Index).

YIELD: 5 CUPS

> **2 pounds fresh blueberries**
> **¹/₂ cup water**
> **2 tablespoons lemon juice**
> **2 cups sugar**
> **4 6-inch sprigs fresh mint**

Pick over the berries, rinse, and combine with water in a heavy, non-reactive 5-quart pan. Cover and bring mixture to a boil. Simmer, uncovered, for 10 minutes.

Add lemon juice, then begin adding sugar ½ cup at a time, allowing the mixture to regain the boil before adding more. Let jam boil for 5 minutes. It will be too thick to reach the jell point on a thermometer, but it will pass the plate test easily.

Pour the jam into a 2-quart measure. Submerge the mint sprigs tied with twine, crushing them against the sides and bottom of the container. Let them steep for 5 minutes, stirring occasionally. Remove the mint.

Fill hot, sterilized jars to within ¼ inch of the lips. Wipe rims clean, attach new lids, and screw caps on tightly. Invert the hot jars momentarily for a quick seal, or process in a boiling water bath, submerged by 1 inch, for 10 minutes.

Boysenberry Jam

The Oregon boysenberries I used in this recipe were oblong and bristling with large, juicy lobes. But, both fresh and cooked, they had a strangely ambivalent taste, favoring neither parent from which they were bred, the raspberry or the blackberry. So I took the initiative and added a little raspberry brandy.

If you enjoy the taste and feel of firm berry bubbles, you will want to eat this jam on warm Buckwheat Muffins or Whole-Wheat English Muffins (see Index).

YIELD: 3 CUPS

> **2 pounds boysenberries**
>
> **$^1/_2$ cup water**
>
> **2 tablespoons lemon juice**
>
> **1$^1/_2$ cups sugar**
>
> **1$^1/_2$ tablespoons raspberry eau de vie**

Combine boysenberries with water in a heavy, non-reactive 5-quart pan. Cover and bring to a boil. Uncover and simmer for 10 minutes.

Add lemon juice, then begin adding sugar $^1/_2$ cup at a time, allowing the mixture to return to a boil before adding more. Continue to cook the jam over medium-low heat for another 12 to 15 minutes, stirring frequently. The liquids will reduce, the jam will thicken, and the temperature will rise to 204° F. Add the eau de vie and cook another minute.

Off heat, pour jam into hot, sterilized jars to within $^1/_4$ inch of the lips. Wipe the rims clean, attach new lids, and screw the caps on tightly. Invert the jars briefly for a quick vacuum seal, or process them in a boiling water bath, submerged by 1 inch, for 10 minutes.

Blueberry Rhubarb Jam

Blueberry and rhubarb offer taste and aroma contrasts that cook into refreshing and quite pleasing preserves. They also leave a lovely tangled texture of silky strands and chewy bits in this jam. Grape-Nuts® Muffins or Drop Scones (see Index) would be my choices to serve with it.

YIELD: 4 CUPS

1 **pound fresh blueberries**

1 **pound rhubarb**

$^1/_3$ **cup water**

$^1/_2$ **tablespoon fresh lemon juice**

2$^1/_2$ **cups sugar**

Zest of 1 lemon

Rinse and pick over the blueberries. Trim and rinse off rhubarb stalks. Cut them into $^1/_2$-inch lengths. Combine fruits in a heavy, non-reactive 4-quart saucepan with water. Cover and bring to a boil. Uncover and simmer for 10 minutes, stirring regularly.

Stir in the lemon juice, then begin adding sugar $^1/_2$ cup at a time, allowing the mixture to return to the simmer before adding more. Continue to cook over medium heat, stirring frequently, for 15 minutes. Partially cover the pot to prevent splattering during the last few minutes of cooking. The temperature should reach 212° F.

Off heat, stir in the lemon zest. Fill hot, sterilized jars to within $^1/_4$ inch of the lips. Wipe the rims clean, attach new lids, and screw caps on tightly. Invert jars briefly for a quick vacuum seal, or process in a boiling water bath, submerged by 1 inch, for 10 minutes.

Peach Pineapple Jam

*Here is another jam in which one fruit with good acidity and an assertive texture—
in this case, the pineapple—flatters the flavor and aroma of a sweet but retiring
partner, the peach. This preserve offers the palate such an interesting texture and
slightly tart finish that a bread with firm or contrasting texture would be welcome.
Try one of the English Muffin recipes, Butter Pecan Muffins, or Tea Brack (see Index).*

YIELD: 4 CUPS

$1^1/_4$ **pounds whole peaches**

2 **tablespoons fresh lemon juice, divided**

$^3/_4$ **pound peeled and cored fresh pineapple**

$1^1/_2$ **cups sugar**

Dip the peaches in boiling water for 30 seconds, then move them to an
iced water bath. When cool enough to handle, peel, halve, and pit them.
Coarsely chop peaches and place them in a heavy, non-reactive 5-quart
pan. Stir in one tablespoon lemon juice to prevent discoloration.

Coarsely chop the pineapple before combining it with the peaches in the
saucepan. Cover and bring fruits to a boil. Uncover and simmer 10 minutes,
stirring regularly. After most of the fruit juices have evaporated, stir in
remaining lemon juice and begin adding the sugar $^1/_2$ cup at a time.
Allow jam to return to the simmer between additions. Cook another
5 minutes over medium heat or until the candy thermometer reads 210° F.

Fill hot, sterilized jars to within $^1/_4$ inch of lips. Wipe the rims clean, attach
new lids, and screw the caps on tightly. Invert the jars briefly for a quick
vacuum seal, or process in a boiling water bath, submerged by 1 inch,
for 10 minutes.

Nectarine Orange Jam

High acidity in both nectarines and oranges makes this a zesty preserve. The cooling effects of fresh mint are especially pleasing here. Grape-Nuts® Muffins and Cream Scones (see Index) taste wonderful with it.

YIELD: 5 CUPS

> 4 **pounds nectarines (7–8 cups peeled, pitted, and sliced)**
> 4 **large navel oranges (1–2 pounds)**
> ¹/₂ **cup water**
> 2 **cups sugar**
> 2 **8-inch sprigs fresh mint (optional)**

Dip the nectarines in simmering water for 30 seconds to loosen their skins. Move them to an iced water bath. When cool enough to handle, halve, pit, and thinly slice them. Place slices in a heavy, non-reactive 8-quart pan.

Remove the zest from 2 oranges with a zester (illustrated on page 13), and add it to the pan. Cut the peels from all the oranges and discard them. Halve the oranges and thinly slice them, removing seeds. Add oranges and water to the nectarines. Cover the pan and bring to a boil. Uncover and simmer until juices are reduced, stirring occasionally. Lower heat if necessary to prevent fruit from sticking to the bottom of the pan. (The mixture will reduce to 6 cups.)

Begin adding sugar ½ cup at a time, allowing the mixture to return to the boil between additions. Continue cooking until the jam thickens and heats to 212° F., about 10 to 12 minutes. Stir frequently but keep the pan partially covered to prevent spatters from escaping.

Pour the jam into a 2-quart measure. Submerge the mint sprigs tied with twine. Crush the mint against the side of the container, and let it steep for 5 minutes. Remove the mint.

Fill hot, sterilized jars to within ¼ inch of the lips. Wipe the rims clean, attach new lids, and screw caps on tightly. Invert momentarily for a quick vacuum seal, or process in a boiling water bath for 10 minutes, submerged by 1 inch.

Ginger Peach Jam

Fresh gingerroot creates just the right exotic perfume and hot sensation on the tongue to provide a memorable accent for sweet peaches. After all, we say "it's ginger peachy" only when everything is just right. This is a jam to savor with English Muffins or Cornmeal Muffins (see Index).

YIELD: 4 CUPS

    3 pounds peaches (6 medium)
    3 slices fresh ginger (size of a quarter)
    1 tablespoon fresh lemon juice
  $^1/_3$ cup water
    2 cups sugar
  $^1/_3$ cup crystallized ginger ($1^1/_2$ ounces)

Dip the peaches in simmering water for 30 seconds, and then submerge them in an iced water bath. When cool enough to handle, peel, halve, and remove pits. Finely chop each peach half by hand or with rapid pulses in a food processor.

Combine peaches with ginger slices, lemon juice, and water in a deep, non-reactive 5-quart saucepan or stock pot. Cover and bring fruit to a boil. Uncover and simmer for 10 minutes. Begin adding sugar ½ cup at a time, allowing the mixture to regain the simmer before adding more.

Continue to simmer the jam, stirring frequently, until the jam thickens and liquids clear. The temperature on a candy thermometer should rise to 212° F. and volume reduce to about 4 cups. Keep the pan partially covered near the end to avoid spatters.

Cut the crystallized ginger into pea-sized pieces. After skimming foam off the jam and removing the ginger slices, fold in the crystallized ginger pieces.

Fill hot, sterilized jars to within $\frac{1}{4}$ inch of the lips. Wipe rims clean, attach new lids, and screw caps on tightly. Quick-seal by inverting the jars briefly, or process in a boiling water bath for 10 minutes, submerged by 1 inch.

Serviceberry and Wild Black Raspberry Jam

The serviceberry tree is found as an understory tree in old-forest growth in temperate areas throughout the United States. Its slender, light gray branches and silver-green leaves often take the shape of a spreading shrub, which is quite distinctive. It also has other names, such as shadbush, shadblow, and Juneberry. This last name refers to the small dark purple berries it produces from June into early July.

Although their taste, fresh from the tree, is sweet and bland, serviceberries develop an enticing bouquet of roses when cooked. Except for this trait, you would never guess that the serviceberry is a member of the rose family. Serviceberries have excellent pectin content and form an inspired partnership with wild, scratchy black raspberries that ripen at the same time in similar wooded settings. Try this jam with English Muffins, Cream Scones, and Tea Brack (see Index).

YIELD: 6 CUPS

- **2 pounds serviceberries**
- **¼ cup water**
- **1 pound black raspberries (4 cups)**
- **2 tablespoons fresh lemon juice**
- **5 cups sugar**

Combine the serviceberries with ¼ cup water in a heavy, non-reactive 5-quart saucepan. Cover and bring to a boil. Uncover and simmer 15 minutes, stirring and crushing the berries to extract their juices. Strain this mixture for 2 hours. There will be about 3 cups of strained juices. If there is more juice, reduce it to 3 cups. If there is less juice, add water to make 3 cups.

Return the serviceberry juice to a clean 5-quart saucepan. Add the black raspberries, cover, and bring mixture to a boil. Uncover and simmer for 10 minutes. Pour in the lemon juice, then begin adding sugar ½ cup at a time, allowing mixture to regain the boil before adding more. Cook jam on medium-high heat, stirring regularly with a long-handled spoon, until it reaches the jell temperature (the boiling temperature on your thermometer plus 8 degrees). This will take about 15 minutes.

Cover the pot when the jam begins to spatter as it nears 220° F. Check the temperature, and stir to reduce the heat every minute or so. Pour the jam into a 2-quart measure. Let it sit, stirring occasionally to redistribute the berries in the jell.

Fill hot, sterilized jars to within ¼ inch of lips. Wipe rims clean, attach new lids, and screw caps on tightly. Either invert each jar briefly for a vacuum seal, or process in a boiling water bath, submerged by 1 inch, for 10 minutes.

Strawberry Kiwifruit Jam

YIELD: 2 CUPS

  1 **pint strawberries, rinsed, stemmed, and halved**

  3 **large kiwifruit, peeled, quartered, and thickly sliced**

$^1/_4$ **cup water**

$^1/_2$ **cup sugar**

Combine both fruits and water in a heavy, non-reactive 4-quart saucepan. Cover the pan and bring fruit to a boil. Uncover and simmer for 10 minutes. Add the $^1/_2$ cup sugar and cook until the liquid is reduced and the jam is thick, about 5 minutes.

Fill hot, sterilized jars to within $^1/_4$ inch of lips. Wipe rims clean, attach new lids, and screw caps on tightly. Either invert each jar briefly for a quick vacuum seal, or process in a boiling water bath, submerged by 1 inch, for 10 minutes.

STRAWBERRY KIWIFRUIT JAM VARIATIONS

Cinnamon Strawberry Kiwifruit Jam

Add one 4-inch cinnamon stick to the pan while cooking the jam. Remove before filling jars.

Strawberry Kiwifruit Jam with Vanilla

Split $^1/_2$ of a large vanilla bean. Scrape out the seeds, and add both the seeds and pod to the pan while cooking the jam. Remove the bean pieces before filling the jars.

Strawberry Kiwifruit Jam with Mint

Add 2, 4-inch stems of fresh spearmint to the completed jam. Crush the stems and leaves on the bottom of the hot pan. Let the herb steep with the jam for 5 minutes. Remove the stems and proceed to fill the jars.

Nectarine Plum Jam with Ginger

YIELD: 3 CUPS

I **pound nectarines (3 cups sliced)**

I **pound red plums (2 $^1/_2$ cups chopped)**

$^1/_3$ **cup water**

2 **slices gingerroot**

I **cup sugar**

Rinse and wipe fruit. Pit and thinly slice the nectarines. Pit and chop the plums. Combine them with water and ginger slices in a non-reactive 4-quart saucepan. Cover the pan and bring mixture to a boil. Uncover and simmer for 10 minutes, stirring frequently, until most of the moisture has evaporated.

Add sugar $^1/_2$ cup at a time, waiting for the liquid to regain the boil before adding more. Cook over medium heat for another 5 minutes, stirring frequently, until the mixture thickens. Remove ginger slices.

Fill hot, sterilized jars to within $^1/_4$ inch of lips. Wipe rims clean, attach new lids, and screw caps on tightly. Either invert each jar briefly for a quick vacuum seal, or process in a boiling water bath, submerged by 1 inch, for 10 minutes.

Strawberry Blackberry Jam

YIELD: 3 ¼ CUPS

1½ pounds strawberries (4 cups halved)

1 pound blackberries

⅓ cup water

½ cup sugar

Rinse, stem, and halve the strawberries. Rinse and drain the blackberries. Combine them with water in a 4-quart non-reactive saucepan. Cover the pan and bring mixture to a boil. Uncover and simmer for 10 minutes. Add sugar and continue to simmer another 5 minutes, stirring more frequently as the jam thickens.

Fill hot, sterilized jars to within ¼ inch of lips. Wipe rims clean, attach new lids, and screw caps on tightly. Either invert each jar briefly for a quick vacuum seal, or process in a boiling water bath, submerged by 1 inch, for 10 minutes.

NO-SUGAR JAMS

If you need to add sugar to preserve fruits, then a jam with no-sugar would seem to be a contradiction. It's not so, however, when you consider that fruit contains its own simple sugar, fructose. We concentrate fructose in no-sugar jams with a simple cooking procedure that produces clean flavors and a pleasing texture. No-sugar jam satisfies a craving for sweets in a totally natural way, which is great news for those who must avoid sucrose for health reasons as well as nutrition-conscious cooks and those who habitually count calories.

With technical considerations at a minimum, the preserver can play with taste and textural combinations. I've given you a number of recipes to start with. You can even vary the texture of the fruits in these recipes a bit, but the consistency will always be thick enough to spread on breads and muffins.

The absence of granular sugar in no-sugar jams highlights exactly how sugar changes fruits when they are cooked together. It's not just the degree of sweetness that is affected. These jams will also lack the sheen that the sucrose gives preserves and a supple coating of the tongue. The taste of a no-sugar jam will also leave the palate with a pleasingly tart finish. They are particularly good combined with breads with nuts and raisins, which lend their natural sweetness to the mix.

To insure their shelf life, I suggest giving all the freshly filled no-sugar jam jars a 10-minute bath submerged in boiling water. They acquire an extra tight seal during this process that protects them from spoilage. This step is optional for all other preserves, where granulated sugar serves as a powerful preservative. Your standard pot for sterilizing jars can be used for this bath. Keep no-sugar jams refrigerated after opening as you would any preserve.

TECHNIQUE FOR MAKING NO-SUGAR JAMS

- Prepare the ingredients for preserving.
- Cook the jams slowly until concentrated, as directed.
- Tightly seal in quilted jars.
- Vacuum seal the preserves as directed.

No-Sugar Peach Pineapple Jam with Apricots

This is a quick, easy recipe, especially if you have a food processor to do the cutting. With such abundant flavor, a light buttery Drop Scone or Risen Biscuit (see Index) would be the perfect complement.

YIELD: 3 CUPS

- 1 1-pound can unsweetened peach pieces and juice
- $1/2$ pound dried apricots, finely chopped
- 1 8-ounce can unsweetened, crushed pineapple in pineapple juice
- 1 4-inch stick cinnamon
- 1 tablespoon fresh lemon juice

Drain peaches and reserve the juices. Dice the peaches by hand or chop with rapid on-and-off motions in a food processor. Cut the apricots to the same size. Combine peach pieces with their juice, and the apricots, the crushed pineapple with juice, and the cinnamon stick in a heavy, non-reactive 4-quart saucepan.

Bring to a boil, reduce heat to simmer, and stir constantly until the apricots are soft, almost all moisture is evaporated, and the jam is thickened. This will take about 10 minutes.

Off heat, stir in lemon juice.

Fill hot, sterilized jars to within $1/4$ inch of the lips. Wipe the rims clean, attach new lids, and screw the caps on tightly. Process jars in a boiling water bath, submerged by 1 inch, for 10 minutes.

No-Sugar Pear and Blueberry Jam

This combination draws together fruits from seasons spanning the summer and early fall months. Its flavor is unexpected and delicious. This preserve is a good stuffing for baked apples and is tasty on Apple Cinnamon Muffins or Buttermilk Currant Scones (see Index).

YIELD: 3 1/2 CUPS

    1 **pound blueberries**
  1/4 **cup water**
1 1/2 **pounds Bartlett pears**
  1/2 **cup unsweetened apple juice concentrate**

Combine blueberries and water in a heavy, non-reactive 4-quart pan. Bring water to a simmer, cover, and cook for 15 minutes. Lift the lid every 5 minutes to make sure the mixture is cooking slowly.

Peel, quarter, core, and dice the pears. Add them to the blueberries with the apple juice. Raise the heat to medium, and let the pears cook and juices reduce over a 15-minute period.

Off heat, spoon jam into hot, sterilized jars to within 1/4 inch of the lips. Wipe the rims clean, attach new lids, and screw caps on tightly. Process jams in a boiling water bath, submerged by 1 inch, for 10 minutes.

No-Sugar Peach Raspberry Jam

This classic combination works well without sugar when you use canned unsweetened peaches, which are less acidic than many fresh varieties. The raspberries, added after the peaches have been reduced, are cooked lightly so their shape and taste remain separate and clear.

Spread this preserve on Zucchini Bread or Butter Pecan Muffins (see Index) for a real breakfast treat.

YIELD: 3 CUPS

2 1-pound cans unsweetened peach halves in juice

8 ounces fresh red raspberries

Drain peaches and finely chop them by hand or with rapid on-and-off motions in a food processor, 1 pound at a time.

Combine peach pieces and juice in a heavy, non-reactive 3-quart saucepan. Bring to a boil, reduce heat to low, and simmer until almost all juice is evaporated from the peaches, stirring frequently. This will take up to 10 minutes. (When the mixture is ready, the bubbles will be small and close together. A spoon scraped across the bottom of the pan will make a hissing sound.)

Off heat, add the raspberries, tossing them into the hot peaches. Cover the pan, return it to low heat, and continue cooking another 5 minutes. Check the jam every minute or so. Shake the pan rather than stir it to redistribute the berries and juices.

Uncover the pan and turn up heat to medium. Stir gently and occasionally until the jam is thickened again, not more than 5 minutes.

Fill hot, sterilized jars to within 1/4 inch of the lips. Wipe the rims clean, attach new lids, and screw the caps on tightly. Process in a boiling water bath, submerged by 1 inch, for 10 minutes.

No-Sugar Apple Grape Jam

Apples and grapes are complementary fruits that hardly ever appear together. Without sugar, their flavors remain naturally tart, and the fresh, spicy gingerroot slices heighten their fruit flavor. Serve Drop Scones and Butter Pecan Muffins (see Index) with this jam.

YIELD: 3 CUPS

3 pounds Macintosh apples

1 12-ounce can unsweetened grape juice

1 cup water

2 slices fresh gingerroot (size of a silver dollar)

Peel, core, quarter, and thinly slice apples. Combine all ingredients in a heavy, non-reactive 4-quart saucepan. Bring to a boil and simmer over low heat for 30 minutes or until the apples are soft and the juice is reduced enough to form a jam-like consistency.

Off heat, remove ginger and fill hot, sterilized jars to within $\frac{1}{4}$ inch of the lips. Tap jars on the counter to force out air pockets in the jam. Wipe the rims clean, attach new lids, and screw the caps on tightly. Process in a boiling water bath, submerged by 1 inch, for 10 minutes.

No-Sugar Apple Blackberry Jam

The choice of a tart, firm apple assures this jam a tangy finish and a texture of chunky fruit nuggets. For a sweeter flavor and softer texture, use Macintosh or Jonathan apples.

You could serve this jam with Grape-Nuts® Muffins or Tea Brack (see Index).

YIELD: 3 CUPS

3 Granny Smith *or* other firm, tart apples ($1^1/_4$ pounds)

1 12-ounce can unsweetened apple juice concentrate

1 pound blackberries

2 4-inch sprigs of fresh, bruised mint (optional)

Peel, quarter, and core the apples. Dice them coarsely and combine them in a 4-quart pan with the apple juice concentrate. Bring the juice to a boil. Regulate the heat to maintain a slow simmer, cover, and cook the apples for 10 minutes.

Add the blackberries to the pan. Return the heat to simmer, cover, and cook for 5 minutes. Uncover, turn the heat up to medium-high, and begin to actively reduce the liquids. Cook until a spoon drawn across the bottom of the pan causes a hissing sound. This will happen within 10 minutes.

Crush the mint stems and add them to the hot jam, off heat. Steep for 5 minutes or until their scent is noticeable. Remove mint and spoon the jam into hot, sterilized jars to within $1/_4$ inch of the lips. Wipe the rims clean, attach new lids, and screw caps on tightly. Process these jams in a boiling water bath, submerged by 1 inch, for 10 minutes.

No-Sugar Cinnamon Nectarine Jam with Pineapple

Combined and reduced with pineapple juice, nectarines attain an intense sweet-sour balance. The cinnamon fragrance seems to sweeten this jam. Butter Pecan Muffins, Cream Scones, and Risen Biscuits (see Index) are all excellent with it. This flavor will also make a refreshing sorbet if you merely dilute it with Simple Syrup (page 244) and freeze it on a sheet-cake pan (see page 223 for Fruit Sorbet recipe).

YIELD: 4½ CUPS

3 **pounds fresh nectarines**

3 **6-ounce cans unsweetened pineapple juice**

1 **cinnamon stick**

Rinse and cut the flesh from the nectarines with skin attached. Cut into ½-inch dice. Combine nectarine pieces with pineapple juice and cinnamon in a heavy, non-reactive 4-quart saucepan. Cover and bring the liquid to a boil; uncover and simmer over medium heat until the jam has thickened. This will take 15 to 20 minutes. As the mixture reduces, begin to stir more frequently to prevent sticking.

Off heat, remove cinnamon stick. Fill hot, sterilized jars to within ¼ inch of the lips. Wipe the rims clean, attach new lids, and screw caps on tightly. Process in a boiling water bath, submerged by 1 inch, for 10 minutes.

No-Sugar Pineapple Raspberry Jam with Apricots

The concentrated sweetness of dried apricots is the catalyst in this combination, balancing the acidity of both of the other fruits. An excellent way to savor the sweet-sour taste harmony and complex texture of this jam is on Cream Scones or Risen Biscuits (see Index).

YIELD: 3 CUPS

- **2 cups unsweetened pineapple juice**
- **12 ounces fresh red raspberries**
- **6 ounces dried apricots, finely chopped**

Combine juice, half the raspberries, and all the apricot pieces in a deep, heavy, non-reactive 4-quart saucepan. Cover the pan and bring to a boil. Uncover and simmer over medium-low heat until almost all the liquid has evaporated, about 10 minutes. Add remaining raspberries. Lower heat, cover the pan, and stew whole berries gently for 5 minutes. Gently shake the pan to determine moisture level, but do not stir. Mixture is ready when almost all moisture has evaporated, about 5 minutes.

Fill hot, sterilized jars to within 1/4 inch of the lips, taking care to keep the soft, whole raspberries intact. Wipe the rims clean, attach new lids, and screw caps on tightly. Process in a boiling water bath, submerged by 1 inch, for 10 minutes.

No-Sugar Blueberry Orange Jam

In this recipe whole blueberries retain their watery sweetness as a distinct, refreshing contrast to the acidic tang of the oranges. This jam is delicious on Oatmeal Muffins and Zucchini Bread (see Index).

YIELD: 3 ⅓ CUPS

3 navel oranges

1 12-ounce can unsweetened orange juice concentrate

1 pound fresh blueberries

Remove the zest from the oranges with a zester (illustrated on page 13). Cut off and discard the inner white peel. Thinly slice the oranges.

Combine juice concentrate, zest, and orange slices in a heavy, non-reactive 4-quart saucepan. Cover and bring to a boil. Uncover and cook on medium-high until most of the liquid is evaporated, 5 to 10 minutes.

Off heat, stir in the blueberries. Cover, reduce the heat to low, and simmer the jam 5 minutes. Uncover and raise the heat. Cook another minute or two, stirring continuously until mixture thickens.

Fill hot, sterilized jars to within ¼ inch of the lips. Wipe the rims clean, attach new lids, and screw caps on tightly. Process in a boiling water bath, submerged by 1 inch, for 10 minutes.

No-Sugar Pear and Grape Jam

This variation of the Pear and Grape Preserves (see Index) has a formidable history. Pear and grape juice, raisoné, as it is called in France, has been made by farmers in Burgundy for several hundred years. A recipe for it first appeared in A. A. Parmentier's early nineteenth-century cookbook in response to a request by Napoleon I for the development of sugar-free foods. (France at that time was being cut off from its sugar supply by an English naval blockade.)

YIELD: 3 CUPS

3 pounds ripe Bartlett pears

1 12-ounce can unsweetened grape juice concentrate

Peel, quarter, and core the pears. Thinly slice the pears and combine with juice concentrate in a heavy, non-reactive 4-quart pan. Cover the pan and bring liquid to a simmer. Uncover and simmer for about 30 minutes until thickened.

Fill hot, sterilized jars to within ¼ inch of the lips. Wipe the rims clean, attach new lids, and screw caps on tightly. Process in a boiling water bath, submerged by 1 inch, for 10 minutes.

No-Sugar Orange Fig Jam

This jam blends intensely sweet dried figs with tart orange juice concentrate and barely cooked fresh orange sections. Drop Scones fresh off the griddle or warm Butter Pecan Muffins (see Index) taste wonderful with this jam.

YIELD: 2 ½ CUPS

8 large dried figs (6 ounces)

1 12-ounce can frozen unsweetened orange juice concentrate

3 navel oranges (1 ½ pounds)

Remove tough stem tips of figs and chop them into ¼-inch dice. Combine them in a heavy, non-reactive 4-quart saucepan with the juice concentrate. Cover the pan and bring to a boil. Cook, uncovered, at a simmer until the mixture thickens, 5 to 10 minutes. Stir steadily after the first 3 minutes. When jam is thick enough, rising bubbles will come to the surface with plopping sounds. Remove pan from the heat.

Slice the peel from the oranges with a knife and discard it. Cut down between the membrane and the pulp to release each segment, discarding membrane. Stir orange pieces into the hot jam. Simmer for another 5 minutes until the jam thickens again.

Fill hot, sterilized jars to within ¼ inch of the lips. Wipe the rims clean, attach new lids, and screw caps on tightly. Process jars in a boiling water bath, submerged by 1 inch, for 10 minutes.

No-Sugar Orange Pineapple Jam

Cloves and allspice berries are brightly flattering spices that tame the acid notes in this fruit combination, but you can experiment with others. Banana Bran Muffins and Oatmeal Muffins (see Index) are good complements to this preserve. It is also very refreshing when diluted with Simple Syrup (page 244) and frozen as a sorbet (see page 223 for Fruit Sorbet recipe).

YIELD: 3 CUPS

- **3 pounds navel oranges (4 cups peeled and coarsely chopped)**
- **1 12-ounce can frozen unsweetened pineapple-orange juice concentrate**
- **2 cups crushed pineapple, after draining**
- **3 whole cloves**
- **4 whole allspice berries**

Combine all fruit ingredients in a heavy, non-reactive 5-quart saucepan. Tie spices in a piece of cheesecloth with cotton twine and stir them into the pan. Cover, and bring mixture to a boil. Uncover and simmer, stirring more frequently as the jam thickens, for as long as 20 minutes.

Off heat, remove spices and fill hot, sterilized jars to within 1/4 inch of the lips. Wipe the rims clean, attach new lids, and screw caps on tightly. Process jars in a boiling water bath, submerged by 1 inch, for 10 minutes.

No-Sugar Apple Strawberry Jam

The addition of sweet woodruff and its fresh scent of newly mown hay adds com-
plexity to this spring jam. Substitute a bag of camomile tea if necessary. It will carry
a sunlit meadow scent to complement the strawberries. This fragrant jam will add
interest and texture to Butter Pecan or Grape-Nuts® Muffins (see Index).

YIELD: 4 CUPS

3 golden Delicious apples

1 12-ounce can unsweetened apple juice concentrate

4 cups strawberries (1 pint)

5 4-inch sprigs of sweet woodruff *or* 1 bag camomile tea

Peel, quarter, and core the apples. Dice them and combine in a heavy, non-reactive 4-quart saucepan with the apple juice concentrate. Cover the pan and bring to a boil. Simmer, partially covered, for 10 minutes. Rinse, stem, and quarter the strawberries. Add them to the pan. Return jam to a simmer, cover, and cook for 5 minutes.

Uncover the pan, turn up the heat to medium-high, and begin to actively reduce the liquid. Cook until a spoon drawn across the bottom of the pan causes a hissing sound. This will happen within 10 minutes.

Off heat, crush the woodruff stems and add them to the hot jam. Steep for 5 minutes. Remove the woodruff stems and ladle jam into hot, sterilized jars to within 1/4 inch of the lips. Wipe the rims clean, attach new lids, and screw the caps on tightly. Process jars in a boiling water bath, submerged by 1 inch, for 10 minutes.

No-Sugar Kiwifruit Pear Jam

YIELD: 2 ½ CUPS

I pound kiwifruit (2^1/$_2$ cups)

4 ounces dried pears (^{3}/$_4$ cup)

8 ounces golden Delicious apples (I^2/$_3$ cups)

^{1}/$_2$ cup water

Peel, quarter, and thinly slice the kiwifruit. Dice the pears. Peel, core, and chop the apple. Combine all the fruit pieces and water in a heavy 5-quart, non-reactive saucepan. Cover and bring mixture to a boil. Uncover and cook at a simmer for 10 minutes. Raise the heat and cook another 2 to 3 minutes, stirring frequently to prevent sticking.

Fill hot, sterilized jars to within ¼ inch of the lips. Wipe the rims clean, attach new lids, and screw caps on tightly. Process jars in a boiling water bath, submerged by 1 inch, for 10 minutes.

No-Sugar Strawberry Pineapple Jam

YIELD: 3 CUPS

1 1-pound can crushed pineapple in unsweetened juice

½ vanilla bean

1 pound fresh strawberries (3⅓ cups)

Pour the pineapple pieces and their juice into a heavy, non-reactive 4-quart saucepan. Score the vanilla bean and scrape out the seeds. Add seeds and bean to the pan. Cover and bring the mixture to a boil. Uncover and simmer for 5 minutes or until most of the juices have evaporated.

Rinse, stem, and quarter the strawberries. Add the berries to the pan, cover, and return the mixture to a boil. Simmer for 5 to 10 minutes to reduce juices, stirring more near the end of the reduction process to prevent sticking.

Off heat, remove the vanilla bean. Fill hot, sterilized jars to within ¼ inch of the lips. Wipe the rims clean, attach new lids, and screw caps on tightly. Process jars in a boiling water bath, submerged by 1 inch, for 10 minutes.

No-Sugar Apple Raspberry Jam

YIELD: 4 CUPS

1 pound golden Delicious apples (3²/₃ cups)

1 6-ounce can unsweetened apple juice

2 ounces dried apple rings

1 pound red raspberries

Scrub, rinse, and wipe dry the apples. Quarter, core, and dice them. Combine the apple pieces with apple juice in a heavy, non-reactive 5-quart saucepan. Cover and bring the mixture to a boil. Uncover and simmer for 5 minutes. Chop up the dried apple rings, and add them to the pan. Cook, stirring frequently, until most of the liquid has reduced.

Rinse the raspberries and stir them into the pan. Cover the pan and bring contents to a boil. Uncover and continue to cook at an active simmer for 3 more minutes or until the jam has thickened, stirring frequently.

Fill hot, sterilized jars to within ¼ inch of the lips. Wipe the rims clean, attach new lids, and screw caps on tightly. Process jars in a boiling water bath, submerged by 1 inch, for 10 minutes.

5 JELLIES

A well made fruit jelly embodies the essence of the pectin jell. Its appearance is clear and inviting in the jar, and it wobbles invitingly when plopped on warm toast and melts smoothly in the mouth, releasing a flood of sweet with sour flavors on the tongue. Homemade jelly convinces the most hurried diner to slow down and savor.

The technique for making jelly is a distillation of fruit-preserving techniques. You feel you are working hand-in-hand with nature throughout the refining process, first cooking fruit, then thoroughly straining pectin-rich juice from skin and pulp, again simmering juices to concentrate pectin, and finally boiling the mixture with sugar to the jell stage. The rhythm of this work is centuries old.

Making jelly is slower than other techniques because of the time required for straining cooked fruit juices through a cheesecloth-lined sieve. The liquid flows rapidly when the fruit is first placed in the strainer, quickly slows to a trickle, then seems to stall out at a slow drip. Don't yield to the temptation to shorten this process. I've discovered that the juices highest in pectin are the last to drip through the sieve! But it is all right to give in to the final great temptation, that of pressing those last few tablespoons through the strainer. The little fruit pulp that could cloud a dark jelly won't be noticeable, although I would take greater care when straining a light-colored juice.

Once you've reduced the fruit juices to the amount specified in the recipe, they are boiled with an equal amount of sugar, added slowly to assure that it dissolves completely and to keep the temperature of the liquid high. One to 2 tablespoons of strained lemon juice, added just before the sugar, facilitates the process. You will have a jelly in 5 to 10 minutes.

The easiest jellies to make are those from fruits and berries blessed with high pectin content such as Concord grapes, black raspberries, cranberries, and red currants. To make other flavors, we use Apple Pectin Stock made from sour apple juice. I offer a variety of flavors for you to master: jelly with wine reductions, with herb infusions, and with vegetable mixes. These jellies can move beyond the breakfast table and become condiments served on a cold meat platter, on a sandwich, or with hors d'oeuvres. I have yet to discover a sandwich that isn't improved by the addition of Hot Pepper Jelly. Once you find a savory use for these sweet condiments, your own creations will evolve.

TECHNIQUE FOR MAKING JELLY

Fruit and Berry Jellies

- Prepare fruit for cooking: coarsely chop larger fruits; remove stems, leaves, and stalks but include cores, pits, or seeds.
- Cook fruit as indicated for 30 minutes, then strain the juices 2 hours.
- Reduce juices as indicated in specific recipes.
- Add sugar to equal the volume of the juices plus lemon juice (if indicated)
- Cook to the jell point.
- Skim the jelly, and pour it into hot sterilized jars.
- Vacuum seal the jelly jars as directed.

Jelly from Apple Pectin Stock

- Prepare apples for cooking: remove stems and coarsely chop; include cores and pits.
- Cook with water for 30 minutes, then strain the juices for 2 hours.
- Reduce juices as indicated in specific recipes.
- Mix with flavoring.
- Add sugar to equal the volume of the Stock plus lemon juice (if indicated).
- Cook to the jell point.
- Skim the jelly, and pour it into hot sterilized jars.
- Vacuum seal the jelly jars as directed.

What do you do when the jelly doesn't set? Check page 19 for first-aid information.

Master Recipe for Grape Jelly

Homemade grape jelly puts the store-bought versions to shame. It jells easily and has an expansive sweet-sour flavor. Banana Bran Muffins and Cream Scones (see Index) make delicious partners for it.

YIELD: 4 ½ CUPS

    4 pounds Concord grapes

  ½ cup water

    4 cups sugar

Rinse grapes and remove the stems. Combine grapes with water in a heavy, non-reactive 4-quart pan. Bring to a boil, slow to a simmer, cover the pot, and cook for 30 minutes. Occasionally stir and crush the grapes against the side of the pan.

Strain juices from the fruit through a cheesecloth-lined sieve for 2 hours. Measure and reduce juices to 4 cups. Bring grape juice to a boil. Add sugar ½ cup at a time, allowing liquid to return to a boil before adding more. Cook to the jell point, which is 8 degrees above the boiling point measured on your thermometer. This will take about 5 minutes. Maintain the boil for a full minute after reaching the jell.

Off heat, skim and ladle into hot, sterilized jelly jars to within ¼ inch of the lips. Wipe the rims clean, attach new lids, and screw caps on tightly. Invert jars briefly to vacuum seal, or process in a boiling water bath, submerged by 1 inch, for 10 minutes.

Grape Jelly with Fresh Thyme

Steep completed jelly in the pan with three 6-inch sprigs of fresh thyme for 5 minutes. Remove thyme and proceed to fill and seal the jars.

Spicy Grape Jelly

Tie one 4-inch cinnamon stick, 4 allspice berries, 4 whole cloves, and 3 cardamom pods in cheesecloth with cotton twine. Cook the spices with the grape juice as the sugar is added. Remove before filling jars.

Crabapple Jelly

The flavor of crabapples can vary quite a bit from one tree to the next, a fact that makes the quality of your jelly hard to predict unless you use fruit from the same tree year after year. Even then, some harvests are better than others. In fact, one attraction of preserving as an annual ritual is its ability to capture the subtle pulse of nature. It's a pleasure to spread this jelly on a hot Butter Pecan Muffin (see Index) and watch it begin to warm and soften just as you eat it.

YIELD: 9 CUPS

5 pounds crabapples

Enough water to cover crabapples (approximately 2 quarts)

Sugar

Stem and halve the apples. Combine them with water in a heavy, non-reactive 8-quart pot. The water should just cover the apples. Bring water to a boil, reduce to a simmer, and cook, partially covered, for 30 minutes. Strain the juice through a cheesecloth-lined sieve for 2 hours.

Measure the juice and set aside an equal volume of sugar. Bring the juices to a boil, and stir in sugar $1/2$ cup at a time, each time waiting for the mixture to return to a boil before adding more.

Cook over medium-high heat until mixture reaches the jell temperature, which is 8 degrees higher than the boiling point measured on your thermometer. This may take as long as 15 minutes. Maintain the boil for a full minute after reaching the jell temperature.

Off heat, skim the jelly and ladle into hot, sterilized jelly jars to within $1/4$ inch of the lips. Wipe the rims clean, attach new lids, and screw caps on tightly. Invert jars briefly to vacuum seal, or process in a boiling water bath, submerged by 1 inch, for 10 minutes.

Cinnamon Cranberry Apple Jelly

Picture this ruby-bright jelly as a beautiful holiday offering with a stick of cinnamon tied in green ribbon around the jar cap. It will taste delicious spread on any rich brioche breads or Christmas stollen. Tea Brack or Butter Pecan Muffins (see Index) would be my serving choices from the breads in this book.

YIELD: 7 CUPS

- **2 pounds cranberries**
- **2 pounds Granny Smith *or* Jonathan apples**
- **6 cups water**
- **Sugar**
- **1 stick cinnamon**

Rinse and pick over the cranberries before weighing them. Coarsely chop the apples, removing stems only. Combine fruits in a heavy, non-reactive 5-quart pan. Pour the water over them and bring to a boil. Reduce heat to a simmer, partially cover, and cook for 20 minutes.

Strain the juice through a cheesecloth-lined sieve for 2 hours.

Add the cinnamon stick to the cranberry-apple juice and bring to a boil in a heavy, 5-quart non-reactive pan. Stir in an equal volume of sugar ½ cup at a time, returning liquid to a boil each time before adding more. Let the jelly boil until it reaches the jell point, which is 8 degrees above the boiling temperature measured on your thermometer. This will take about 5 minutes. Maintain the boil for a full minute after reaching the jell point.

Off heat, skim the jelly and ladle into hot, sterilized jelly jars to within ¼ inch of the lips. Wipe the rims clean, attach new lids, and screw caps on tightly. Invert jars briefly to vacuum seal, or process in a boiling water bath, submerged by 1 inch, for 10 minutes.

Black Raspberry Jelly

This luxurious jelly will flatter any bread or biscuit, particularly a chewy English Muffin (see Index).

YIELD: 3 CUPS

    4 pints black raspberries (3 pounds)
$^1/_2$ cup water
    3 cups sugar
    1 tablespoon fresh lemon juice

Pick over and rinse the berries. Combine them with water in a heavy, non-reactive 5-quart saucepan. Cover and bring to a boil. Simmer, partially covered, for 10 minutes, stirring and crushing the berries against the side of the pan. Strain the juice through cheesecloth for 2 hours.

Measure the berry juice and reduce to 3 cups or add water to measure 3 cups. Bring juice to a boil in a heavy, non-reactive 5-quart pan. Add the lemon juice, then the sugar $^1/_2$ cup at a time, allowing the liquid to return to a boil each time before adding more. Let the liquid boil until it reaches the jell temperature, which is 8 degrees above the boiling temperature measured on your thermometer. This should happen within 10 minutes.

Off heat, skim the jelly and ladle into hot, sterilized jelly jars to within $^1/_4$ inch of the lips. Wipe the rims clean, attach new lids, and screw caps on tightly. Invert jars briefly to vacuum seal, or process in a boiling water bath, submerged by 1 inch, for 10 minutes.

Master Recipe for Red Currant Jelly

This is the quintessential jelly, with its exquisitely tart flavor, bright ruby color, and shimmering jell. It flatters rich breads and muffins as a preserve and makes a great poaching medium and sauce for peaches, pears, and apples. My favorite bread partners for this vigorous jelly are Buckwheat Muffins and Whole–Wheat English Muffins (see Index).

YIELD: 5 ¼ CUPS

4 pounds red currants

Sugar

Pick over and rinse the currants. Combine them with water in a heavy, non-reactive 5-quart saucepan. Cover and bring to a simmer. Cook, uncovered, slowly for 10 minutes, stirring and crushing the berries against the side of the pan. Strain the mixture through a cheesecloth-lined sieve for 2 hours.

Measure the currant juice, then place it in a 4-quart saucepan and bring to a boil. Stir in an equal volume of sugar ½ cup at a time, allowing the liquid to return to a boil each time before adding more. Bring liquid to jell temperature, which is 8 degrees above the boiling temperature measured on your thermometer. This will take up to 10 minutes. Maintain the boil for a full minute after reaching the jell.

Off heat, skim the jelly and ladle into hot, sterilized jelly jars to within ¼ inch of the lips. Wipe the rims clean, attach new lids, and screw caps on tightly. Invert jars briefly to vacuum seal, or process in a boiling water bath, submerged by 1 inch, for 10 minutes.

Red Currant Jelly with Cardamom

**Bouquet garni: 1, 2-inch stick cinnamon;
10 cardamom pods, bruised to expose the seeds**

Add the spices tied in a cheesecloth to the strained currant juices. Proceed with the master recipe. Remove spices just before completed jelly is poured into jars.

Sweet and Hot Currant Jelly

YIELD: 3 CUPS

2$^1/_2$ cups red currant juice

1 tablespoon jalapeño chile, seeds removed, diced

2$^1/_2$ cups sugar

Combine the currant juice with chili pepper pieces in the bowl of a food processor or blender. Pulse for 15 seconds to fragment and infuse the juice with the chile oils. Proceed to make jelly as described above in the Master Recipe for Red Currant Jelly.

Apple Pectin Stock

With a supply of this apple juice concentrate, you can make virtually any jelly flavor you desire. The pectin in the apple will contribute generously to a jell; its subtle fragrance will defer to the scents of other fruits, herbs, and spices. To avoid being caught short, make more than one recipe of stock when time allows, and store it , vacuum-sealed, in your larder or freeze it. Fresh stock will refrigerate for up to two weeks.

YIELD: 3 CUPS

4 pounds Granny Smith apples

8 cups water

Stem the apples and coarsely chop them. Place pieces in a heavy, non-reactive 5-quart pan; include seeds, skins, and cores. Pour in 8 cups water. Bring to a boil, reduce heat to a simmer, and cook, partly covered, for 30 minutes. Stir the pan once or twice, turning the apples at the top into the simmering liquid.

Strain mixture through a damp cheesecloth-lined sieve for 1 hour. There will be about 8 cups of apple juice. Begin to reduce this juice in a 5-quart pan while continuing the straining process for another hour. The last cup of juice has a higher pectin level than the juices strained initially. Add this late juice to the juices reducing in the pan. Reduce to 3 cups total.

If you are going to use the stock within the next 2 weeks, simply pour it into a clean storage jar and refrigerate. Stock can also be frozen in clean plastic containers.

To vacuum-seal the stock, fill hot, sterilized jars to within ¼ inch of the lips. Wipe the rims clean, attach new lids, and screw caps on tightly. Invert jars briefly to vacuum seal, or process in a boiling water bath, submerged by 1 inch, for 10 minutes.

Pectin Stock Using Greening Apples

YIELD: 4 CUPS

4 pounds greening apples

2 quarts water

Follow the directions for Apple Pectin Stock above, but cook the apples and water for only 20 minutes. You want them to exude their juices but not to cook into applesauce.

This apple variety will strain out to about 1 cup juice per pound of apples. There is no need to reduce this stock.

Apple Puree for Muffins, Waffles, and Pancakes

After straining off all the apple juice, run the pulp and skin through a food mill fitted with a medium-fine screen. The resulting unsweetened apple-sauce can be refrigerated up to a month and used to flavor baked goods.

Chardonnay Jelly

Jellies made from good-quality varietal wines with a fruity scent and good acid, such as cabernet sauvignon and chardonnay, are particularly flavorful. Since the jelling action is provided by the pectin stock alone, you are free to experiment with different flavors. For example, why not reduce a red wine with a bouquet of your favorite spices for a mulled wine jelly? Tea Brack, Zucchini Bread, and Cream Scones (see Index) pair well with this tart jelly.

YIELD: 2 ½ CUPS

- 1 **bottle (750 ml) French chardonnay wine (a white Burgundy)**
- 1 **recipe (p. 103) Apple Pectin Stock (3 cups)**
- 2 **tablespoons fresh lemon juice, strained**
- 2 **cups sugar**

Reduce the wine to 1 cup in a heavy, non-reactive 4-quart pan. Reserve the wine, and rinse out the pan. Combine pectin stock, wine, and lemon juice in this pan, bring to a simmer, and reduce by half to 2 ½ cups. Add the sugar ½ cup at a time, allowing liquid to return to a boil each time before adding more. Continue to boil until mixture reaches the jell temperature, which is 8 degrees above the boiling temperature measured on your thermometer. This will take 5 to 10 minutes.

Off heat, skim the jelly and ladle into hot, sterilized jelly jars to within ¼ inch of the lips. Wipe the rims clean, attach new lids, and screw caps on tightly. Invert jars briefly to vacuum seal, or process in a boiling water bath, submerged by 1 inch, for 10 minutes.

Cabernet Jelly

Identical to the recipe above with the exception of the wine used. Substitute a bottle of cabernet sauvignon for the chardonnay.

Kir Cocktail Jelly

If you want to transform your favorite wine aperitif into a jelly, plan to experiment with small batches until you get the right flavor balance. This particular combination of white wine and crème de cassis has a delicate grape taste and the aroma of black currants. It is delicious with a Cream Scone or Grape–Nuts® Muffin (see Index).

YIELD: 2 ½ CUPS

- **1 bottle (750 ml) dry white wine (sauvignon blanc preferred)**
- **3 tablespoons crème de cassis**
- **1 recipe (p. 103) Apple Pectin Stock (3 cups)**
- **2 cups sugar**

Reduce wine over high heat to 1 cup in a heavy, non-reactive 4-quart pan. Stir in the crème de cassis and Apple Pectin Stock. Reduce this mixture by half to 2 cups.

Bring liquid to a boil in a heavy, non-reactive 5-quart pan, and add the sugar ½ cup at a time, returning it to a boil each time before adding more. Continue to cook at a boil until liquid reaches the jelling temperature, which is 8 degrees above the boiling temperature measured on your thermometer. This will take about 5 minutes.

Off heat, skim the jelly and ladle into hot, sterilized jelly jars to within ¼ inch of the lips. Wipe the rims clean, attach new lids, and screw caps on tightly. Invert jars briefly to vacuum seal, or process in a boiling water bath, submerged by 1 inch, for 10 minutes.

Mint Jelly

The warm perfume of fresh herbs in scented jelly will flood your senses with memories of a summer garden. Herb fragrances are evocative but fragile, so I spread this jelly on simple, buttery Cream Scones or Risen Biscuits (see Index).

YIELD: 3 ½ CUPS

- **1 recipe (p. 103) Apple Pectin Stock (3 cups)**
- **2 tablespoons fresh lemon juice, strained**
- **4 4-inch sprigs of fresh mint**
- **3 cups sugar, warmed**

Bring Apple Pectin Stock and lemon juice to a boil in a heavy, 5-quart, non-reactive pan. Carefully rinse and pat dry the mint stems. Bind them with kitchen twine, crush the bundle to bruise the leaves, and stir them into the hot apple juice. Add sugar to the bubbling juice ½ cup at a time, allowing it to return to a boil each time before adding more.

After all the sugar is added, continue to simmer, and test with a candy thermometer until it reaches the jell temperature, which is 8 degrees above the boiling temperature measured on your thermometer. This will take 5 minutes at most.

Off heat, skim the jelly and ladle into hot, sterilized jelly jars to within ¼ inch of the lips. Wipe the rims clean, attach new lids, and screw caps on tightly. Invert jars briefly to vacuum seal, or process in a boiling water bath, submerged by 1 inch, for 10 minutes.

Sweet Pepper Jelly

The sweet, woodsy fragrance of bell peppers blends well with apple stock in this recipe. It also makes a beautiful jelly, full of swimming bits of bright pepper gems. This is a delicious jelly to take along on a late summer picnic with Cornmeal Muffins, Risen Biscuits, or Whole-Wheat English Muffins (see Index).

YIELD: 4 CUPS

I cup minced red and green bell peppers

I recipe (p. 103) Apple Pectin Stock (3 cups)

3 cups sugar

Zest of I lemon

Remove stems, interior seeds, and membranes from the peppers. Mince the flesh and add it to the pectin stock in a heavy, non-reactive 4-quart pan. Bring this to a simmer.

Begin adding the sugar ½ cup at a time, allowing the liquid to return to a boil each time before adding more. After all the sugar is added, let the jelly boil until it reaches the jell point, which is 8 degrees above the boiling temperature measured on your thermometer. This will take about 5 minutes. Maintain the boil for a full minute after reaching the jell.

Off heat, stir in the lemon zest and pour into a quart-sized glass measure. Skim the jelly well and let it sit for 10 minutes, stirring occasionally to distribute the pepper pieces throughout the jelly.

Ladle jelly into hot, sterilized jars to within ¼ inch of the lips. Wipe the rims clean, attach new lids, and screw caps on tightly. Invert jars briefly to vacuum seal, or process in a boiling water bath, submerged by 1 inch, for 10 minutes.

Hot Pepper Jelly

A little hot pepper goes a long way in fragrant apple stock. To tame this hot jelly, spread it on cooled Cornmeal Muffins or Buckwheat Muffins (see Index). If there is cream cheese to slather on in place of butter, so much the better.

YIELD: 4 ½ CUPS

$^1/_2$ **cup chile peppers (any mixture jalapeño, serrano, red chilies)**

1 **recipe (p. 103) Apple Pectin Stock (3 cups)**

2 **tablespoons strained fresh lemon juice**

3 **cups sugar**

Halve the chilies lengthwise and remove the seeds, but keep the white inner membrane intact. Finely mince enough chilies to measure ½ cup.

Combine chile pieces with the apple stock in a heavy, non-reactive 4-quart pan. Bring liquid to a boil and add the lemon juice. Begin adding sugar ½ cup at a time, letting mixture return to a boil each time before adding more. Let the mixture boil until it reaches the jell point, which is 8 degrees above the boiling point measured on your thermometer. This may take up to 15 minutes. Maintain the boil for a full minute after reaching the jell.

Pour the jelly into a quart measure. Skim the jelly and let it sit for 10 minutes, stirring occasionally to distribute the pepper pieces throughout the jelly.

Ladle jelly into hot, sterilized jelly jars to within ¼ inch of the lips. Wipe the rims clean, attach new lids, and screw caps on tightly. Invert jars briefly to vacuum seal, or process in a boiling water bath, submerged by 1 inch, for 10 minutes.

Rosemary Red Onion Jelly

Onions make a wonderful and unusual presence cooked with Apple Pectin Stock. As the jelly cooks, tender onion rings form an appealing web of circles firmly suspended in lovely amber. The preserve tastes fully of onions with a mild jelly finish, qualities flattering to both breads and cold meats.

Try this preserve on Oatmeal, Buckwheat, or Cornmeal Muffins as well as the Whole-Wheat English Muffins (see Index). It is also delicious served with cold roast pork, smoked ham, and roast beef.

YIELD: 3 ½ CUPS

> **1 pound red onions**
>
> **1 recipe (p. 103) Apple Pectin Stock (3 cups)**
>
> **3 tablespoons fresh lemon juice**
>
> **Sugar**
>
> **2 teaspoons rosemary leaves, finely chopped**

Peel the onions and trim off the root ends. Thinly slice them in a food processor or by hand with a V-slicer (mandoline). Combine onion slices and Apple Pectin Stock in a heavy, non-reactive 5-quart pan. Bring liquid to a boil. Reduce the heat to a simmer and cook, partially covered, for 10 minutes.

Strain the stock from the onion slices for 10 minutes. Measure the stock and set aside an equal volume of sugar. Return the juice and onion slices to a clean pan. Stir in the lemon juice, bring mixture to a simmer, and begin adding the sugar ½ cup at a time, allowing the liquids to return to a boil each time before adding more sugar. After all the sugar is added, boil until the jelly reaches the jell point, which is 8 degrees above the boiling point measured on your thermometer. This will take 10 to 15 minutes. Boil jelly a full minute at the jell point.

Pour the hot jelly into a 1-quart glass measure. Stir in the minced rosemary pieces, and allow the mixture to stand for 10 minutes, stirring occasionally.

Ladle the jelly into hot, sterilized jars to within $\frac{1}{4}$ inch of the lips. Wipe the rims clean, attach new lids, and screw caps on tightly. Invert the jars briefly for a quick vacuum seal, or process in a boiling water bath, submerged by 1 inch, for 10 minutes.

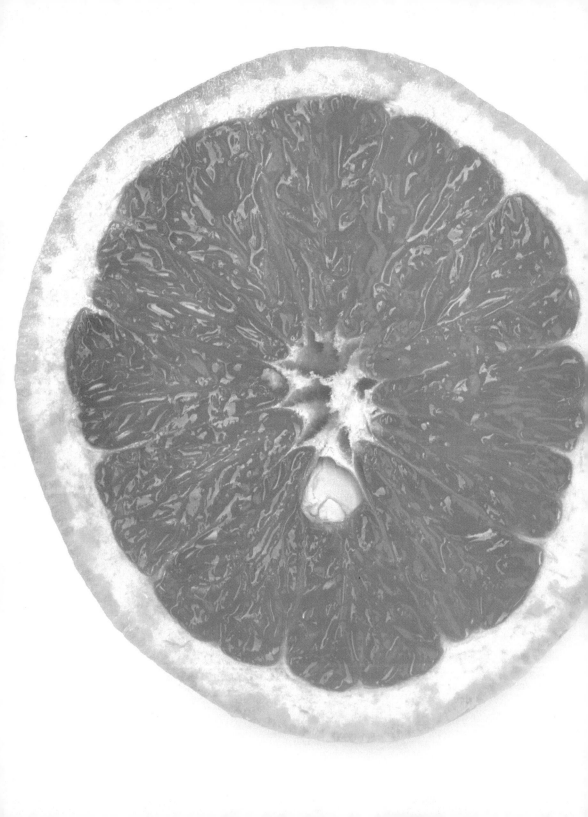

6 MARMALADES

The first marmalade recipe to appear in an English cookbook was named for a popular Portuguese preserve, *marmelado*, in 1524. It was made with the marmelo quince, a hard, astringent raw fruit that mellows as it cooks into a soft sauce with an intense apple scent.

Today's marmalades—shimmering jellies with suspended bits of bitter citrus pulp and peel—are altogether different. Early on, English marmalade became identified with the fiercely bitter Seville orange from Spain. English recipes for bitter orange marmalade were commonplace in the 17th century, but the version made commercially by Scotsman James Keiller and his wife popularized it in the 18th century.

A rival story about the history of marmalade links it to Mary Queen of Scots. According to this account, Mary consumed French marmalade to combat seasickness returning to Scotland from Calais. This condiment became known in her retinue as a pun on her name, *"Marie malade,"* rather than its French title, *cotignac*. Marmalade quickly grew to be a popular restorative in the 16th century during Mary's time. Its ingredients then included oranges and medicinal herbs. Wouldn't a fruit preserve marketed as a royal cure, rich in antioxidants, potent herbs, and bearing a French name become an instant hit even today?

I would not go so far as to suggest any curative powers for marmalade in the 21st century unless we count pure eating pleasure as therapy. My response to marmalade's blend of sweet, sour, and bitter sensations is complete satisfaction. The recipes that follow explore an artful blend of bitter citrus peel with fruit and sugar to create a variety of intense flavors. I also add summer vegetables and spices to citrus jells in several recipes. Why not try the complex taste experience of Ratatouille Marmalade with grilled meat at a summer barbecue or with a sharp Cheddar cheese on toast?

In addition to its bitter flavor, there are two other important reasons for including the bitter peel of a citrus fruit in marmalade. First, the white inner peel is the main source of pectin in citrus fruit. Secondly, floral oils in the outer rind of citrus fruits give each its distinctive scent. Here's how it works in your mouth. When you taste marmalade, its sweet and sour elements affect the taste sensors at the front of your tongue. You next experience the bitter sensations in the back. At the same time, floral aromas of citrus oil flood your nose and the back of your soft palate with fragrance. It's a uniquely gratifying experience.

My enthusiasm for the nuanced taste of marmalade led me through many enjoyable experiments. I share my discoveries with you in this collection. Most recipes contain lemon, which is my tribute to the original bitter Seville orange. Let me remind you to select a navel rather than a thin-skinned juice orange when preparing any of these marmalades that call for oranges.

A standard procedure in all the marmalade recipes is the addition of a volume of water equal to the volume of the fruit and peel. The presence of water softens the harsh bitterness of the peel. It is joined by fruit juices and citrus oil during cooking. These proportions provide a rich jelly for the suspended fruit pieces in the finished preserve.

TECHNIQUE FOR MAKING QUICK MARMALADE*

- Clean and cut up the fruit and peel.
- Measure the combined fruit, and add an equal volume of cool water.
- Cook and reduce this mixture as directed in the recipe.
- Add the same volume of sugar to the simmering base, as directed.
- Cook to the jell stage.
- Let the finished marmalade sit, off the heat, for 5 minutes.
- Stir the marmalade occasionally to redistribute the citrus peel.
- Fill jars and process as directed.

TECHNIQUE FOR MAKING TWICE-COOKED MARMALADE*

- Clean and cut up the fruit and peel.
- Measure the combined fruit, and add an equal volume of cool water.
- Some recipes call for a portion of the inner peel of the fruit to be tied in cheesecloth and added.
- Cook the fruit and water 15 minutes the evening before, and leave the base to steep overnight.
- Remove the cheesecloth bag of peels if used.
- Measure the cooked volume. Reduce if directed in the recipe.
- Add sugar in the same volume as the base, as directed.
- Cook to the jell stage.
- Let the finished marmalade sit, off the heat, for 5 minutes.
- Stir the marmalade occasionally to redistribute the citrus peel.
- Fill jars and process as directed.

* Twice-cooked marmalades are more complex and delicate-tasting than the quick variety.

Thirty-Minute Orange Marmalade

YIELD: 4 CUPS

6 navel oranges

Sugar

Halve and press enough oranges to collect 1 ½ cups fresh juice.

Scrub the skins of remaining oranges after removing labels and brand imprints. Quarter the oranges and roughly chop. Place pieces in a food processor with ½ cup orange juice, and pulse until the pulp resembles a coarse puree. You should have about 1 quart of juice, pulp, and peel.

Combine contents of processor with remaining juice in a heavy, non-reactive 5-quart saucepan. Cover and bring to a boil. Uncover and simmer, stirring frequently, until the mixture is dry. Measure this volume and set aside an equal volume of sugar.

Return orange mixture to a boil and add sugar, ½ cup at a time, continuing to boil until the temperature reaches the jell point, which is 8 degrees above the boiling temperature as measured on your thermometer. This should take place within 5 minutes. Off heat, pour into a 1-quart Pyrex© measure to cool for 10 minutes, stirring occasionally.

Pour marmalade into hot, sterilized jars to within ¼ inch of the rims. Wipe the rims clean, attach new lids, and screw caps on tightly. Invert the jars briefly to vacuum seal, or process in a boiling water bath, submerged by 1 inch, for 10 minutes.

Quick Pink Grapefruit Marmalade with Vanilla

YIELD: 3 ½ CUPS

1 large, thin-skinned pink grapefruit

Water

1 vanilla bean

3 cups sugar

Scrub, rinse, and wipe the grapefruit dry. Quarter it, remove seeds, and finely chop with rapid pulsing action in the work bowl of a food processor. Measure the pulp and combine the fruit with an equal volume of water in a 4-quart non-reactive saucepan.

Score the vanilla bean and scrape out the seeds. Add seeds and pod to the grapefruit mixture. Cover and bring to a boil. Uncover and simmer until reduced to 3 cups

Begin adding sugar, ½ cup at a time, allowing the marmalade to regain a boil before adding more sugar. Continue to cook until the marmalade reaches the jell point, which is 8 degrees above the boiling temperature measured on your thermometer. This will take 5 to 10 minutes.

Pour the marmalade into a quart measure to cool for 5 minutes. Remove the vanilla bean pieces and stir to redistribute the peel. Pour marmalade into hot, sterilized jars to within ¼ inch of the rims. Wipe the rims clean, attach new lids, and screw caps on tightly. Invert the jars briefly to vacuum seal, or process in a boiling water bath, submerged by 1 inch, for 10 minutes.

Quick-Mixed Citrus Marmalade

YIELD: 5 ½ CUPS

1 **thin-skinned pink grapefruit**

1 **navel orange**

1 **seedless lemon (smooth skinned)**

1 **lime**

Water

5 **cups sugar**

Scrub, rinse, and wipe the fruits dry. Cut the grapefruit into 8 pieces, removing seeds. Repeat with the orange. Combine citrus pieces in the work bowl of a food processor and rapidly pulse until finely chopped. Halve and thinly slice the lemon and lime. Measure this total fruit base and combine with an equal volume of water in a non-reactive 8-quart pan. Cover and bring to a boil. Uncover and simmer for 20 minutes or until the mixture is reduced to 5 cups.

Begin adding sugar, ½ cup at a time, stirring after each addition and allowing the mixture to regain a simmer. After all the sugar has been added, continue boiling for 10 minutes or until the marmalade thickens and clings to a metal spoon. This super-thick marmalade will not boil up as much as the thinner ones. The temperature may not reach the jell point, but it will pass the spoon and cold-plate test. Remove from the heat before fruit pieces begin to stick to the bottom of the pan.

Off heat, pour into a 2-quart glass measure. Pour marmalade into hot, sterilized jars to within ¼ inch of the rims. Wipe the rims clean, attach new lids, and screw caps on tightly. Invert the jars briefly to vacuum seal, or process in a boiling water bath, submerged by 1 inch, for 10 minutes.

Quick Orange Cranberry Marmalade

A preserve rich in oranges and cranberries comes in handy for many occasions, from Thanksgiving through the Christmas holiday. It also makes a memorable sweet-sour filling for a dessert tart garnished with fresh orange slices. You could even use it as a relish with turkey or ham. Wouldn't it also make a delightful holiday gift? Butter Pecan Muffins and Cream Scones (see Index) are my favorite breads with this preserve.

YIELD: 3 CUPS

3 medium navel oranges (1 pound)

Water

2 cups cranberries

3 cups sugar

Scrub the oranges and finely chop one in the work bowl of a food processor with rapid pulsing action. Cut peel from the other two oranges. Reserve the peel of one orange in a cheesecloth bag; discard remaining peel. Halve and thinly slice the peeled oranges. Measure the chopped orange, orange slices, and orange peel and pour an equal volume of water into a heavy, non-reactive 5-quart pan. Add the chopped and sliced orange and bag of orange peels to the pan, cover, and bring mixture to a boil. Uncover and simmer for 15 minutes.

Pick over and discard bruised cranberries before measuring them. Rinse them, add them to the orange mixture, cover the pan, and return mixture to a simmer. Cook for 10 minutes, stirring regularly. Measure and reduce this marmalade base to 3 cups. Remove the cheesecloth bag and squeeze out the juices into the base.

Return to a boil and stir in the sugar ½ cup at a time, allowing mixture to return to a boil each time before adding more. Continue to cook until the marmalade reaches the jell point, which is 8 degrees above the boiling temperature measured on your thermometer. This will take 5 to 10 minutes.

Pour the marmalade into a 1-quart measure, and let it sit for 5 minutes, stirring down the fruit pieces occasionally. Pour into hot, sterilized jelly jars to within $\frac{1}{4}$ inch of the rims. Wipe the rims clean, attach new lids, and screw caps on tightly. Invert jars briefly to vacuum seal; or process in a boiling water bath, submerged by 1 inch, for 10 minutes.

Spicy Pink Grapefruit Marmalade

Zesty is the best way to describe this quick marmalade. The bitter finish results from the presence of inner white peel that is cooked only once. Try this intensely flavorful preserve on English Muffins with Yogurt, Buckwheat Muffins, or Risen Biscuits (see Index).

YIELD: 4 CUPS

2 thin-skinned pink grapefruits

Water

Bouquet Garni: 2 star anise, 5 allspice berries, 1 4-inch cinnamon stick

3$^1/_2$ cups sugar

Night Before

Scrub and rinse the grapefruits. Quarter one and thinly slice. Remove the outer zest from the other, using a stripper tool. Cut off and discard remaining peel; quarter and thinly slice the pulp.

Measure the fruit pieces and combine them with an equal volume of cool water in a heavy, non-reactive 5-quart pan. Wrap the bouquet garni in cheesecloth and submerge it in the pan. Cover and bring the mixture to a boil. Uncover and simmer for 15 minutes. Put a lid on the pan and leave at room temperature overnight.

Next Day

Measure the marmalade mix. Return to a boil and reduce to 3$^1/_2$ cups.

Stir the sugar into the simmering grapefruit mixture $^1/_2$ cup at a time, allowing mixture to return to a boil each time before adding more. Keep marmalade at a boil until it reaches the jell point, which is 8 degrees higher than the boiling temperature measured on your thermometer. This will take 5 to 10 minutes.

Pour the marmalade into a 1-quart measure and let it sit for 5 minutes, stirring occasionally. Remove the cheesecloth spice bag. Pour into hot, sterilized jelly jars to within ¼ inch of the rims. Wipe the rims clean, attach new lids, and screw caps on tightly. Invert jars briefly to vacuum seal; or process in a boiling water bath, submerged by 1 inch, for 10 minutes.

Orange Marmalade I

This is the first of two twice-cooked marmalade recipes. I enjoy it most on warm breads with contrasting flavors and scents, such as the Apple Cinnamon Muffins and Banana Bran Muffins (see Index).

YIELD: 5 CUPS

2 medium navel oranges
1 medium lemon
   Water
4 cups sugar

Night Before
Scrub and quarter oranges lengthwise. Cut each quarter in half, then halve the remaining pieces. Continue cutting into coarse dice by hand or chop them, using rapid on-and-off motions, in a food processor. Transfer to a measuring cup.

Peel the lemon, halve it, and thinly slice the pulp, removing all seeds. Measure all the fruit pieces and combine them with an equal volume of cool water in a heavy, non-reactive 5-quart pan. Cover and bring to a boil. Uncover and simmer for 15 minutes. Cool to room temperature, cover, and let stand overnight.

Next Day
Measure the marmalade base, return it to the pan, and reduce it to 4 cups. Begin adding sugar, 1/2 cup at a time, to the reduced mixture, allowing it to return to a boil after every addition before adding more. Allow the marmalade to boil until it reaches the jell temperature, which is 8 degrees above the boiling temperature measured on your thermometer. This will take 5 to 10 minutes.

Pour the marmalade into a 2-quart measure and let it sit for 5 minutes, stirring down the fruit pieces occasionally. Pour the marmalade into hot, sterilized jelly jars to within 1/4 inch of the rims. Wipe the rims clean, attach new lids, and screw caps on tightly. Invert jars briefly to vacuum seal; or process in a boiling water bath, submerged by 1 inch, for 10 minutes.

Orange Marmalade II

In this second marmalade recipe, much of the bitter inner peel from the oranges and lemons is discarded. As a result, the preserve has to be reduced more before it will jell.

YIELD: 3 CUPS

> **2 navel oranges**
> **1 medium lemon**
> **Water**
> **2^1/$_2$ cups sugar**

Night Before
Scrub the oranges and lemons. Use a stripper tool (illustrated on page 13) to remove 15 strips of peel from the oranges. Place strips in a 1-quart measure. Peel all fruit and cut off the remaining inner white pith, reserving 1 cup of this pectin material in a cheesecloth bag. Discard the rest of the peel and pith. Quarter and thinly slice the oranges and lemons, removing all seeds.

Measure the combined peel strips and fruit. Place them in a heavy, non-reactive 5-quart pan with an equal volume of water. Add the bag of pectin-rich pith and bring to a boil. Cover and again bring to a boil. Uncover and simmer for 15 minutes. Cool, cover, and let mixture stand at room temperature overnight.

Next Day
Remove the cheesecloth bag from the cooled liquid. Squeeze retained juices into the marmalade base. Discard the bag. Measure the marmalade base and simmer until reduced to 2 ½ cups.

Add the sugar ½ cup at a time, allowing the pan to return to a boil each time before adding more. Let the marmalade boil until it reaches the jell temperature, which is 8 degrees higher than the boiling temperature measured on your thermometer. This will take 10 to 12 minutes. Maintain a boil for a full minute after reaching the jell point.

Pour the marmalade into a 1-quart measure and let it sit for 5 minutes, stirring down the fruit pieces occasionally. Pour into hot, sterilized jelly jars to within ¼ inch of the rims. Wipe the rims clean, attach new lids, and screw caps on tightly. Invert jars briefly to vacuum seal; or process in a boiling water bath, submerged by 1 inch, for 10 minutes.

Citrus Marmalade with Star Anise

When you want a subtle blend of your favorite winter fruits, this is the citrus marmalade you are looking for. The strips of peel are colorful and tangy; the jelly is firm and flavorful. It tastes wonderful on a chewy English Muffin (see Index).

YIELD: 4 ½ CUPS

1 **pink grapefruit ($^3/_4$ pound)**

2 **medium navel oranges ($^3/_4$ pound)**

1 **lemon (4 ounces)**

Water

1 **tablespoon star anise**

4 **cups sugar**

Night Before

Scrub the citrus fruits and cut the grapefruit into 8 pieces, removing seeds. Finely chop these pieces in the work bowl of a food processor with rapid pulsing action. Cut 16 strips of peel from the oranges and lemon, using a stripping tool. Cut off the remaining peel from these fruits and discard it. Halve the fruits, remove seeds, and thinly slice.

Measure the grapefruit pieces, orange and lemon slices, and peel strips, and combine them with an equal volume of water in a heavy, non-reactive 5-quart pan. Add the star anise tied in a cheesecloth bag. Cover and bring the mixture to a boil. Uncover and simmer for 15 minutes. Cool to room temperature, cover, and let the mixture sit overnight at room temperature.

Next Day

Measure the marmalade base. Reduce the base to 4 cups and begin adding sugar, ½ cup at a time, returning mixture to a boil each time before adding more. Cook until marmalade reaches the jell point, which is 8 degrees above the boiling temperature measured on your thermometer. This will take less than 10 minutes.

126

Pour the marmalade into a 1-quart measure and let it sit for 5 minutes, stirring occasionally. Remove the bag of star anise, and stir down the fruit pieces. Pour into hot, sterilized jelly jars to within ¼ inch of the rims. Wipe the rims clean, attach new lids, and screw caps on tightly. Invert jars briefly to vacuum seal; or process in a boiling water bath, submerged by 1 inch, for 10 minutes.

Lime Vanilla Marmalade

YIELD: 3 ¼ CUPS

1 pound fresh limes

1 vanilla bean

Water

Sugar

Night Before
Scrub and peel the limes with a paring knife. Thinly slice the peel pieces. Halve and thinly slice the fruit, removing all seeds. Measure the volume of sliced peel and fruit (about 2 cups), and add them and an equal volume of water to a heavy, non-reactive 5-quart pan.

Split open the vanilla bean and scrape out the seeds. Add the seeds and pod to the pan. Cover and bring to a boil. Uncover, reduce to a simmer, and cook steadily for 10 minutes. Let this cool to room temperature, cover, and let stand overnight.

Next Day
Measure fruit mixture, and set aside an equal volume of sugar. Bring mixture to a boil. Add the sugar, ½ cup at a time, allowing the liquid to return to a boil each time before adding more. Boil until marmalade reaches the jell point, which is 8 degrees above the boiling point measured on your thermometer. This will happen within 10 minutes.

Pour the marmalade into a 1-quart measure and let it sit for 5 minutes, stirring occasionally. Stir down the fruit pieces. Pour the mixture into hot, sterilized jelly jars to within ¼ inch of the rim. Wipe the rims clean, attach new lids, and screw caps on tightly. Invert jars briefly to vacuum seal; or process in a boiling water bath, submerged by 1 inch, for 10 minutes.

Lemon Lime Marmalade with Cinnamon

Limes and lemons offer distinctly different flavors. One cannot be substituted for the other in food or drink without a noticeable alteration in taste. Yet this marmalade proves they are not incompatible. A blend of their unique qualities creates a new and most delicious taste harmony. Lemon Lime Marmalade is delicious on Zucchini Bread and Whole-Wheat English Muffins (see Index).

YIELD: 4 ½ CUPS

- **2 large lemons**
- **2 limes**
- **Water**
- **Sugar**
- **1 cinnamon stick**

Night Before
Scrub the fruits and trim the outer peel from lemons and limes with a vegetable peeler (illustrated on page 13). Cut the peel into thin strips. Cut off the inner white peel from all fruits, reserving the lemon peels in a cheesecloth bag and discarding the lime peels. Thinly slice the fruits and combine with the zest.

Measure the fruit and peel and add it with an equal volume of water to a heavy, non-reactive 5-quart pan. Add the cinnamon stick and cheesecloth bag of lemon peels. Cover and bring to a boil. Uncover and simmer for 15 minutes. Let the mixture cool to room temperature, cover, and let stand overnight at room temperature .

Next Day
Remove the cheesecloth bag and squeeze out juice into the marmalade base before discarding bag. Measure fruit and liquid and set aside an

129

equal volume of sugar. Bring mixture to a boil and add sugar, ½ cup at a time, waiting for the liquid to return to a boil each time before adding more. Cook until marmalade reaches the jell point, which is 8 degrees above the boiling temperature measured on your thermometer. This will take 5 to 10 minutes.

Pour the marmalade into a 1-quart measure, and let it sit for 5 minutes, stirring occasionally. Remove the cinnamon stick. Stir down the fruit pieces.

Ladle mixture into hot, sterilized jars to within ¼ inch of the rims. Wipe the rims clean, attach new lids, and screw caps on tightly. Invert jars briefly to vacuum seal; or process in a boiling water bath, submerged by 1 inch, for 10 minutes.

Lemon Ginger Marmalade

The dynamic sensations of sweet, sour, and bitter in lemons combined with hot and aromatic ginger make this a marmalade that wakes up taste buds and flatters almost any bread. Tea Brack and English Muffins (see Index) are particularly good with it. This preserve can also be transformed into a spectacular Lemon Amaretto Soufflé (see page 226).

YIELD: 4 CUPS

1 pound lemons

3 slices fresh ginger

   Water

   Sugar

Night Before
Scrub and quarter lemons lengthwise. Remove seeds and thinly slice, leaving peel intact. Measure lemon pieces and ginger slices, and cover with an equal volume of cool water in a heavy, non-reactive 5-quart pan. Cover and bring lemon mixture to a boil. Uncover and simmer for 15 minutes. Let the mixture cool to room temperature, cover, and let stand overnight at room temperature.

Next Day
Measure the marmalade base. Return to a simmer and add an equal volume of sugar, ½ cup at a time, allowing mixture to return each time to a boil before adding more. Continue cooking until mixture reaches the jell point, which is 8 degrees above the boiling temperature measured on your thermometer. This will happen within 10 minutes.

Pour the marmalade into a 2-quart measure and let it sit for 5 minutes, stirring occasionally. Stir down the fruit pieces. Pour into hot, sterilized jelly jars to within ¼ inch of the rims. Wipe the rims clean, attach new lids, and screw caps on tightly. Invert jars briefly to vacuum seal; or process in a boiling water bath, submerged by 1 inch, for 10 minutes.

131

Citrus Marmalade with Apricots

Dried apricots add a sweet accent and toothsome texture to sour citrus ingredients, which is quite pleasing to the palate. This marmalade would taste wonderful on warm Buckwheat Muffins or English Muffins (see Index).

YIELD: 6 CUPS

6 ounces dried apricots

1 thin-skinned pink grapefruit (1 pound)

1 lemon ($^{1}/_{4}$ pound)

1 medium navel orange ($^{1}/_{2}$ pound)

Water

5 cups sugar

Night Before
Coarsely chop the apricots and reserve.

Scrub the citrus fruit and strip 15 pieces of peel from the grapefruit and lemons with a stripper tool. Cut remaining peel from the fruits and discard. Thinly slice the fruit. Cut the orange into 8 pieces, and finely chop it in the work bowl of a food processor with a rapid pulsing action.

Combine and measure the fruit slices, citrus strips, orange pieces, and apricots. Place this mixture in a heavy, non-reactive 5-quart saucepan with an equal volume of water. Cover and bring to a boil. Uncover and simmer for 15 minutes. Let mixture return to room temperature, cover, and let stand overnight at room temperature.

Next day
Measure the marmalade mixture and reduce to 5 cups. Begin adding sugar, $^{1}/_{2}$ cup at a time, allowing the mixture to return each time to a boil before adding more. Continue cooking until it reaches the jell point, which is 8 degrees above the boiling point measured on your thermometer. This will take 5 to 10 minutes.

Pour the marmalade into a 2-quart measure and let it sit for 5 minutes, stirring occasionally. Stir down the fruit pieces. Pour into hot, sterilized jelly jars to within $\frac{1}{4}$ inch of the rims. Wipe the rims clean, attach new lids, and screw caps on tightly. Invert jars briefly to vacuum seal; or process in a boiling water bath, submerged by 1 inch, for 10 minutes.

Red Bell Pepper Marmalade

A bell pepper's natural sweetness lends a distinctive taste to the blended citrus ingredients. No spices are specified here, but ginger or cinnamon, even bay leaves, would make an interesting addition. Cornmeal Muffins and English Muffins with Yogurt (see Index) would add texture and an interesting scent to this marmalade, eaten warm for breakfast or with soup for supper.

YIELD: 4 ½ CUPS

1 large red bell pepper

1 navel orange

1 lemon

  Water

4 cups sugar

  Optional seasoning: 3 slices fresh ginger

Night Before

Rinse pepper. Holding it upright by the stem, cut the sides from the fruit, leaving behind the core of seeds and membrane. Thinly slice these "side" pieces into thin julienne strips.

Scrub, rinse, and dry the orange and lemon. Cut the orange into 8 pieces, and quarter the lemon. Finely chop the citrus by hand or with repeated pulses in the work bowl of your food processor.

Measure the combined pepper slices and orange-lemon mixture. Pour this base, an equal volume of water, and the optional ginger slices into a heavy, non-reactive 5-quart pan. Cover and bring to a boil. Uncover and simmer for 15 minutes. Let mixture cool to room temperature, cover, and let sit overnight.

Next Day

Bring marmalade base to a boil and reduce to 4 cups. Stir in the sugar, ½ cup at a time, returning the pan to a boil each time before adding more sugar. Continue to boil until it reaches the jell point, which is 8 degrees above the boiling temperature measured on your thermometer. This will take about 10 minutes. Maintain a boil for a full minute after reaching the jell point.

Pour the marmalade into a 2-quart measure and let it sit for 5 minutes, stirring occasionally. Remove the ginger pieces (if used), and stir down the pepper pieces. Pour the marmalade into hot, sterilized jelly jars to within ¼ inch of the rims. Wipe the rims clean, attach new lids, and screw caps on tightly. Invert jars briefly to vacuum seal; or process in a boiling water bath, submerged by 1 inch, for 10 minutes.

Apple and Onion Marmalade

Apples and onions are frequently paired as a garnish for pork, liver, and cabbage dishes, and they complement each other here. Lemon seemed the natural citrus partner for them in a marmalade. You'll find this textured preserve delicious with Buckwheat Muffins or Grape-Nuts® Muffins (see Index) and as a condiment with cold pork or roast beef.

YIELD: 5 CUPS

2 lemons

2 medium Granny Smith apples

1 small red onion

Water

4 cups sugar

6 stems fresh spearmint

Night Before
Scrub the lemons. Use a vegetable peeler (illustrated on page 13) to remove the outer, colored peel from the lemons. Slice these strips into thinner strips ⅛ inch wide. Cut off the remaining peel and the white inner pith. Tie these in cheesecloth bag and reserve. Halve the peeled lemons and thinly slice them, removing seeds as necessary. Combine lemon strips and pulp in an 8-cup measure.

Scrub, quarter, and core the unpeeled apples. Thinly slice the quarters. (They may be chopped into coarse dice with rapid on-and-off pulses in the food processor.) Add these to the measure.

Peel and thinly slice the onion. Place the onions on top of the apples in the measuring cup. Combine this mixture with an equal volume of water in a heavy, non-reactive 5-quart pan. Submerge the cheesecloth bag of lemon rinds. Cover and bring to a boil. Uncover and simmer for 15 minutes. Let the mixture cool to room temperature, cover, and let sit overnight at room temperature.

Next Day

Before discarding it, squeeze juices from the cheesecloth bag into the pan. Measure the marmalade base and reduce it over high heat to 4 cups.

Stir in the sugar, ½ cup at a time, waiting for the mixture to return to a boil each time before adding more. Continue to boil until the jell point is reached, usually within 10 minutes. Maintain a boil for a full minute after you establish the jell.

Pour the marmalade into a 2-quart measure. Add the mint stems and leaves tied with string. Crush the mint against the sides and bottom of the container. Let the mint steep in the marmalade for 10 minutes, stirring occasionally. Remove the mint and pour marmalade into hot, sterilized jars to within ¼ inch of the rims. Wipe the rims clean, attach new lids, and screw caps on tightly. Invert jars briefly to vacuum seal; or process in a boiling water bath, submerged by 1 inch, for 10 minutes.

Lime Zucchini Marmalade

Slim, firm zucchini no more than 6 inches long are the best for grating into this mild and fragrant preserve. The dark green and white flecks they leave suspended in jelly will be most tender and flattering to the citrus fruits and seasonings. Lime Zucchini Marmalade is a delicious addition to a batch of Oatmeal Muffins or Risen Biscuits (see Index).

YIELD: 5 CUPS

> **2 small zucchini (8–10 ounces total)**
> **3 limes (¹/₂ pound)**
> **Water**
> **1 bay leaf**
> **1 3-inch stick cinnamon**
> **4 cups sugar**

Night Before
Rinse and trim ends from the zucchini. Coarsely grate them. Scrub, dry, halve, and thinly slice the limes. Combine grated squash and lime slices in a 1-quart measure. Combine this base, an equal volume of water, the bay leaf, and the cinnamon stick in a heavy, non-reactive 5-quart pan. Cover and bring to a boil. Uncover and simmer for 15 minutes. Cool this mixture to room temperature, cover, and let sit overnight.

Next Day
Measure and reduce the marmalade base to 4 cups. Add sugar to the mixture, ¹/₂ cup at a time, returning the liquid to a boil each time before adding more. Cook until the marmalade reaches the jell temperature, which is 8 degrees above the boiling temperature measured on your thermometer. This will take up to 10 minutes. Maintain the boil for a full minute after reaching the jell point.

Pour the marmalade into a 2-quart measure and let it sit for 5 minutes, stirring occasionally. Remove the bay leaf and cinnamon. Stir down the fruit pieces, and ladle the mixture into hot, sterilized jars to within ¼ inch of the rims. Wipe the rims clean, attach new lids, and screw caps on tightly. Invert jars briefly to vacuum seal; or process in a boiling water bath, submerged by 1 inch, for 10 minutes.

LEMON ZUCCHINI MARMALADE VARIATION

Lemon Zucchini Marmalade with Basil

Substitute ½ pound lemons for the limes. Eliminate the bay leaf and cinnamon stick. Stir 2 tablespoons of finely minced fresh basil leaves into the marmalade after pouring it into the 2-quart measure.

Orange Zucchini Marmalade

Small, tender zucchini sliced into thin rings is as wonderful with oranges as it is with limes in the Lime Zucchini Marmalade. This time the texture is bolder and so is the taste—after the introduction of tangy sections of fresh gingerroot. Why not try this preserve with Zucchini Bread (see Index) for more of a good thing?

YIELD: 4 ½ CUPS

 2 **small zucchini (2 cups grated)**
 2 **navel oranges (2 cups chopped)**
 1 **quart water**
 3 **quarter-sized pieces fresh ginger**
 4 **cups sugar**

Night Before
Rinse off and trim ends of the zucchini. Coarsely grate it. Scrub the oranges and cut each into 8 pieces. Chop oranges finely by hand or coarsely pulverize with pulsing action in the work bowl of the food processor. Measure the combined zucchini and orange. Place this mix with an equal volume of water and the ginger slices in a heavy, non-reactive 5-quart pan. Cover the pan and bring to a boil. Uncover and simmer for 15 minutes. Cool to room temperature, cover, and let mixture sit overnight.

Next Day
Measure and reduce the mixture to 4 cups. While at the boil, begin adding sugar, ½ cup at a time, returning liquid to a boil ech time before adding more. Continue to boil until the mixture reaches the jell temperature, which is 8 degrees above the boiling temperature measured on your thermometer. This will take about 10 minutes. Maintain a boil for a full minute after reaching the jell point.

Off heat, remove ginger slices. Let the marmalade sit in the pan for 5 minutes. Stir down the fruit pieces, and ladle mixture into hot, sterilized jars to within ¼ inch of the rims. Wipe the rims clean, attach new lids, and screw caps on tightly. Invert jars briefly to vacuum seal; or process in a boiling water bath, submerged by 1 inch, for 10 minutes.

Citrus and Green Pepper Marmalade

The summer bell peppers, winter citrus, and festive seasonings make this marmalade a year-long favorite on brunch buffets and at barbecue picnics. It will taste great on fresh-baked Risen Biscuits and Cornmeal Muffins (see Index).

YIELD: 3 ½ CUPS

- **1 large navel orange**
- **1 lemon**
- **1 green bell pepper**
- **Water**
- **Bouquet Garni: 2 cloves, 2 allspice berries, 10 fennel seeds, 1 bay leaf**
- **4 cups sugar**

Night Before
Scrub and wipe dry the orange and lemon. Quarter each, remove seeds from the lemon, and cut all quarters in half. Finely chop the citrus pieces with rapid pulsing action in the work bowl of a food processor. Rinse the pepper. Holding it upright by the stem, cut the sides from the fruit, leaving behind the core of seeds and membrane. Thinly slice these end pieces into julienne strips.

Measure the volume of pepper slices and citrus pulp. Combine this base with an equal volume of cool water in a heavy, non-reactive 5-quart pan. Add the spices tied in a cheesecloth bag. Cover the pan and bring mixture to a boil. Uncover and simmer for 15 minutes. Let mixture cool, cover, and let sit overnight.

Measure the volume of the marmalade base. Bring it to a boil and reduce to 4 cups. Add sugar, ½ cup at a time, waiting for the marmalade to return to a boil each time before adding more. Continue to boil until it reaches the jell point, which is 8 degrees above the boiling temperature measured on your thermometer. This will take 10 to 15 minutes.

Pour the marmalade into a 1-quart measure, and remove the bouquet garni. Let mixture sit for 5 minutes, stirring occasionally. Stir down the fruit pieces, and ladle the mixture into hot, sterilized jars to within ¼ inch of the rims. Wipe the rims clean, attach new lids, and screw caps on tightly. Invert jars briefly to vacuum seal; or process in a boiling water bath, submerged by 1 inch, for 10 minutes.

Ratatouille Marmalade

A classic ratatouille blend of zucchini, tomato, onion, and green pepper becomes a rich marmalade balanced between sweet and sour ingredients. The lemons provide a tart taste that is brought into equilibrium by the sugar.

This is a preserve meant for a serious breakfast table or a picnic spread and can be served with steamy hot Risen Biscuits and Buckwheat English Muffins (see Index). A vegetable marmalade is also good with cold leftover roasts and spicy sausages.

YIELD: 5 ½ CUPS

1 **cup thinly sliced red onion**

1 **small zucchini**

1 **small green bell pepper**

1 **Italian plum tomato**

2 **lemons (12 ounces)**

Water

6 **cups sugar**

4 **teaspoons fresh lemon juice**

Night Before

Slice the onion and coarsely grate the zucchini. Remove stem, seeds, and membranes from the pepper before thinly slicing. Dip the tomato in boiling water for 30 seconds. Cool under running water and slip off the skin. Halve, seed, and coarsely chop the tomato.

Scrub and wipe dry the lemons. Quarter them and remove seeds. Halve the quarters and finely chop them with rapid pulsing action in the work bowl of your food processor. Measure the combined fruit and vegetable pieces. Place them in a heavy, non-reactive 5-quart pan with an equal volume of cool water. Cover and bring mixture to a boil. Uncover and simmer for 15 minutes. Let mixture cool to room temperature, cover it, and let stand overnight.

Next Day

Measure the marmalade base. Bring mixture to a boil and reduce to 6 cups. Begin adding sugar, ½ cup at a time, waiting for the mixture to return to a boil each time before adding more. Add the lemon juice and continue to boil until the marmalade reaches the jell point, which is 8 degrees above the boiling temperature measured on your thermometer. This will take about 15 minutes. Maintain a boil for a full minute after reaching the jell point.

Pour the marmalade into a 2-quart measure and let it sit for 5 minutes, stirring occasionally. Stir down the fruit pieces, and ladle marmalade into hot, sterilized jelly jars to within ¼ inch of the rims. Wipe the rims clean, attach new lids, and screw caps on tightly. Invert jars briefly to vacuum seal; or process in a boiling water bath, submerged by 1 inch, for 10 minutes.

7 PRESERVES

When I began testing recipes for this chapter more than twenty years ago, I was determined to create a new kind of fruit preserve. My goal was to suspend whole berries and fruit pieces in a natural jell rather than the traditional super-sweet sugar syrup. The procedure I developed combines both jelly technique and a steeping period adapted from the older-style preserving method.

My hybrid process involves cooking fruit, then straining and boiling juices with sugar to create a jelly. The reserved cooked fruit pieces are then added back into the jelly to steep. The jelly, with its fruit pieces, is boiled again briefly with a small amount of sugar and lemon juice. Another quarter cup of sugar and an additional tablespoon of lemon juice is added during the second, short boil.

The consistency of these jelled preserves varies from firm, when natural pectin is high, to soft-set jell in the lower-pectin fruits. It's a consistency that will easily hold its shape on a slice of toast and also cascade attractively down a scoop of ice cream in a dish.

Ever since the Romans stored figs in honey, the term fruit preserves has been synonymous with whole or large pieces of fruit suspended in a sugar syrup. The traditional French process described in *LaRousse Gastronomique* is one of multiple poachings. Fruits are cooked and cooled in a sugar syrup so that the juices they exude when heated are reabsorbed as they cool. Repeated cooking and cooling gradually mingles juices and syrup to the point where the density of the juices inside the fruit is the same as that of the surrounding liquid, causing the fruit to hang suspended in the poaching medium. It's safe to say that the oldest technique for making a preserve did not employ a pectin jell.

I created "Quick" preserves recipes (which you will find at the beginning of the chapter) that eliminate the jelly and steeping steps and use either natural or commercial pectin. Fruits and berries with high pectin levels are cooked for 10 minutes, measured, and boiled with sugar to the jell point. For fruits with weaker pectin levels, I ask you to strain fruit juices after the initial cooking and add a small amount of commercial pectin. Fruit and enhanced juice are then brought back to a boil, sugar is added, and the mixture is cooked to jell stage.

TECHNIQUE FOR MAKING PRESERVES

Quick Preserves

- Prepare the fruit or berries for cooking.
- Simmer the fruit for 10 minutes to release the pectin.
- High pectin fruits: measure the volume of cooked fruit and juice.
- Low pectin fruits: strain and measure the juices; add commercial pectin as indicated; recombine with fruit pieces.
- Cook the fruit and juices with the specified amounts of sugar and lemon juice.
- Cook preserve to the jell point.
- Allow the preserve to sit for 10 minutes, stirring occasionally, so that the fruit pieces can become evenly distributed in the preserve.
- Vacuum seal the preserves as directed.

Soft-Set Jell

- Prepare the fruit or berries for cooking.
- Simmer the fruit for 10 minutes to release the pectin.
- Strain the juices. Cook to concentrate if indicated. Reserve the fruit pieces.
- Cook the juices with specified amounts of sugar and lemon juice to the jell stage.
- Stir the cooked fruit into the jelly and steep for 15 minutes.

- Cook to the jell point with a small amount of lemon juice and sugar as directed in the recipe.
- Allow the preserve to sit for 5 minutes, stirring occasionally, so that the fruit pieces can become evenly distributed in the preserve.
- Vacuum seal the preserves as directed.

Quick Strawberry Preserves

YIELD: 3 $\frac{1}{2}$ CUPS

> 2 **pounds fresh strawberries**
>
> $\frac{1}{2}$ **cup water**
>
> 3 **tablespoons Sure-Jell®**
>
> 1$\frac{1}{2}$ **tablespoons lemon juice**
>
> 3 **cups sugar**

Rinse, drain, and hull the berries. Leave small fruit whole and halve or quarter large berries so pieces are of uniform size. Place berries and water in a deep, non-reactive 8-quart pan. Cover pan and bring to a simmer, stirring occasionally to avoid sticking. Simmer, uncovered, for 10 minutes. Strain juices for 10 minutes and measure them. Reserve the fruit pieces. If there is more or less than 2 cups of juice, either add water or reduce juices to that amount. Stir in the Sure-Jell® until dissolved and then the lemon juice.

Combine the strawberry juices and reserved berries in a clean saucepan and return to a boil. Begin adding sugar, $\frac{1}{2}$ cup at a time, allowing the mixture to return to a boil each time before adding more. Continue cooking until the liquid nears the jell point, 216 – 218° F. This will take 5 to 10 minutes. Preserves will be quite thick and sheet heavily from a metal spoon.

Off heat, pour the preserve into a 1-quart mixing bowl and allow it to sit for 10 minutes, stirring occasionally to redistribute the berries in the jelly. Fill hot, sterilized jars to within $\frac{1}{4}$ inch of the rims. Wipe the rims clean, attach new lids, and screw the caps on tightly. Invert the jars briefly for a quick vacuum seal; or process in a boiling water bath, submerged by 1 inch, for 10 minutes.

Quick Red Raspberry Preserves

YIELD: 3 CUPS

4 pints raspberries (1$^{1}/_{2}$ pounds)

$^{1}/_{3}$ cup water

2 tablespoons lemon juice

Sugar

Rinse and drain the berries. Combine with water in a heavy, non-reactive 5-quart pan. Cover and bring to a simmer. Uncover and simmer for 10 minutes. Measure the volume of fruit and juices. Set aside the same volume of sugar.

Return the mixture to a boil and add the lemon juice. Add sugar, $^{1}/_2$ cup at a time, allowing the mixture to return to a boil each time before adding more. Continue cooking until the liquid reaches 218° F. This will take 5 to 7 minutes. Preserves will be quite thick and sheet heavily from a metal spoon.

Off heat, pour the preserve into a 1-quart mixing bowl and allow it to sit for 10 minutes, stirring occasionally to redistribute the berries. Fill hot, sterilized jars to within $^{1}/_4$ inch of the rims. Wipe the rims clean, attach new lids, and screw the caps on tightly. Invert the jars briefly for a quick vacuum seal; or process in a boiling water bath, submerged by 1 inch, for 10 minutes.

Quick Blackberry Preserves with Lemon Zest

YIELD: 3 ½ CUPS

4 pints (1½ pounds) blackberries

⅓ cup water

Grated zest from 1 lemon

Sugar

Rinse and drain the berries. Combine with water in a heavy, non-reactive 5-quart pan. Cover and bring to a simmer. Uncover and simmer for 10 minutes. Measure the volume of fruit and juices. Set aside the same volume of sugar.

Return the mixture to a boil and add the lemon zest. Add sugar, ½ cup at a time, allowing the mixture to return to a boil each time before adding more. Continue cooking until the liquid reaches 218° F. This will take 5 to 10 minutes. Preserves will be quite thick and sheet heavily from a metal spoon.

Off heat, pour the preserve into a 1-quart mixing bowl and allow it to sit for 10 minutes, stirring occasionally to redistribute the berries. Fill hot, sterilized jars to within ¼ inch of the rims. Wipe the rims clean, attach new lids, and screw the caps on tightly. Invert the jars briefly for a quick vacuum seal; or process in a boiling water bath, submerged by 1 inch, for 10 minutes.

Quick Tropical Pineapple Preserves

YIELD: 4 ½ CUPS

4 cups fresh pineapple pieces (1 pineapple, peeled and cored)

1½ cups water

1 vanilla bean

2 tablespoons Sure-Jell®

2 tablespoons lemon juice

2½ cups sugar

Cut top and bottom ends from the pineapple. Quarter it lengthwise and remove the peel and core. Slice quarters into 6 lengthwise slices. Cut across these slices at ¼-inch intervals to make thin wedges. Combine pineapple pieces with water in a heavy, non-reactive 5-quart pan, cover, and bring to a simmer. Halve the vanilla bean lengthwise and scrape out the seeds. Add seeds and pod to the pineapple, uncover pan, and simmer for 10 minutes.

Strain the fruit mixture for 5 minutes. Reserve the fruit pieces. Reduce liquid to 2 cups if there is excess, or add water to measure 2 cups if there is less. Whisk in the Sure Jell® and lemon juice. Recombine the pineapple pieces and liquid in a clean 5-quart pan and return to a simmer.

Add sugar, ½ cup at a time, allowing the mixture to return to a boil each time before adding more. Continue cooking until the liquid reaches 218° F. This will take about 10 minutes. Preserves will sheet heavily from a metal spoon.

Off heat, pour the preserve into a 1-quart mixing bowl and allow it to sit for 10 minutes, stirring occasionally to redistribute the pineapple pieces. Fill hot, sterilized jars to within ¼ inch of the rims. Wipe the rims clean, attach new lids, and screw the caps on tightly. Invert the jars briefly for a quick vacuum seal; or process in a boiling water bath, submerged by 1 inch, for 10 minutes.

Quick Pineapple Lemon Preserves

This is a beautiful golden preserve full of engaging pineapple strands. Lemon juice balances the sugar and emphasizes the pineapple's flavor. Try this preserve with Risen Biscuits, Banana Bran Muffins, or Cream Scones (see Index). It also makes a great topping for cheesecake (see Index), substituting a vanilla wafer crust for the Pecan Sandies and nuts (see Index for Blueberry Pecan Cheesecake recipe).

YIELD: 4 CUPS

I pineapple (4 cups cut up)
Zest and juice of 2 lemons
2 cups water
3 tablespoons Sure-Jell®
3 cups sugar

Cut top and bottom ends from the pineapple. Quarter it lengthwise and remove the skin and core. Slice quarters into 6 lengthwise slices. Cut across these slices at ¼-inch intervals to make thin wedges. (If you prefer to use a food processor, cut pineapple quarters into 8 pieces and chop 2 quarters at a time with rapid on-and-off action to make ¼-inch bits.) Use a zester (illustrated on page 13) to remove the thin outer peel from two lemons. Halve and juice the lemons.

Combine pineapple pieces, lemon zest, lemon juice, and water in a heavy, non-reactive 8-quart pan. Cover and bring liquid to a boil, reduce heat to a simmer, uncover, and cook for 15 minutes.

Strain the juices for 15 minutes. Reserve the pineapple pieces. Reduce the strained juices to 3 cups or add water to measure that amount. Stir in the Sure-Jell®.

Combine the juices and reserved pieces of fruit in a clean 5-quart pan and return to a simmer. Stir in the sugar, ½ cup at a time, allowing the liquid to return to a boil each time before adding more. Continue cooking on high heat for 10 minutes or until the temperature rises to 216° F. and the preserve passes the cold plate and spoon tests.

Off heat, allow the preserve to rest for 10 minutes, stirring occasionally to redistribute the fruit pieces. Ladle preserves into hot, sterilized jars to within ¼ inch of rims. Wipe the rims clean, attach new lids, and screw caps on tightly. Invert jars briefly for a quick vacuum seal; or process in a boiling water bath, submerged by 1 inch, for 10 minutes.

Quick Pear Preserves with Pernod

YIELD: 6 CUPS

- **3 pounds Bartlett pears (7 cups)**
- **2 cups water**
- **4 tablespoons fresh lemon juice, divided**
- **3 tablespoons Sure-Jell®**
- **4 cups sugar**
- **3 tablespoons Pernod**

Peel, core, and chop the pears into ½-inch pieces. Combine with water and 2 tablespoons lemon juice in a non-reactive 8-quart pan. Cover and bring mixture to a simmer; uncover and cook for 10 minutes. Strain the juices and reserve the pear pieces.

Measure the juices, reduce to 3 cups if necessary, and whisk in the Sure-Jell® and remaining 2 tablespoons of lemon juice. Recombine the pear pieces and juices in a clean pan. Return to a boil and stir in the sugar, ½ cup at a time, returning the liquid to a boil each time before adding more. Continue to boil until the preserve reaches the jell point, which is 8 degrees above boiling temperature as measured on your thermometer. Stir in the Pernod and cook for 30 seconds longer.

Off heat, pour the preserve into a 2-quart mixing bowl and allow it to sit for 10 minutes, stirring occasionally to redistribute the pear pieces. Fill hot, sterilized jars to within ¼ inch of the rims. Wipe the rims clean, attach new lids, and screw the caps on tightly. Invert the jars briefly for a quick vacuum seal; or process in a boiling water bath, submerged by 1 inch, for 10 minutes.

Quick Pear and Grape Preserves

YIELD: 6 CUPS

3 pounds Bartlett pears (7 cups)

1 cup water

Juice of 1 lemon

1 12-ounce can frozen unsweetened grape juice concentrate

4 tablespoons Sure-Jell®

4 cups sugar

Peel, core, and cut the pears into ½-inch pieces. Combine them in a non-reactive 8-quart pan with lemon juice and water. Cover and bring mixture to a simmer. Uncover and cook for 10 minutes. Strain the juices and reserve the pear pieces. Add the grape juice concentrate. Reduce juices, if necessary, to 4 cups. Stir in the Sure-Jell®.

Return the juices and reserved pieces of fruit to a clean 8-quart pan. Bring to a boil and begin adding sugar, ½ cup at a time, returning the liquid to a boil each time before adding more. Continue to boil until the preserve reaches the jell point, which is 8 degrees above boiling temperature as measured on your thermometer. This should take about 10 minutes.

Off heat, pour the preserve into a 2-quart mixing bowl. Allow the preserve to sit for 10 minutes, stirring occasionally to redistribute the pear pieces. Fill hot, sterilized jars to within ¼ inch of the rims. Wipe the rims clean, attach new lids, and screw the caps on tightly. Invert the jars briefly for a quick vacuum seal; or process in a boiling water bath, submerged by 1 inch, for 10 minutes.

Quick Cherry Cassis Preserves

YIELD: 3 CUPS

2 pounds pitted, tart cherries (4 cups)

$^1/_3$ cup water

$^1/_3$ cup Crème de Cassis

3 tablespoons Sure-Jell®

Juice of $^1/_2$ lemon

3 cups sugar

Combine the cherries and water in a heavy, non-reactive 5-quart pan. Cover and bring to a simmer. Uncover and cook for 10 minutes. Strain the juices. Reserve the cherries.

Bring the Cassis to a simmer in a non-reactive skillet. Flame the boiling liqueur to release any residual alcohol. Pour into the cherry juices. Stir the Sure-Jell® and lemon juice into the juices.

Recombine the cherries and juices in a clean saucepan and return to a boil. Begin adding sugar, $^1/_2$ cup at a time, returning the liquid to a boil each time before adding more. Continue to boil until the preserve reaches the jell point, which is 8 degrees above boiling temperature as measured on your thermometer. This should take about 10 minutes.

Off heat, pour the preserve into a 2-quart mixing bowl. Allow the preserve to sit for 10 minutes, stirring occasionally to redistribute the cherry pieces. Fill hot, sterilized jars to within $^1/_4$ inch of the rims. Wipe the rims clean, attach new lids, and screw the caps on tightly. Invert the jars briefly for a quick vacuum seal; or process in a boiling water bath, submerged by 1 inch, for 10 minutes.

Blueberry Blackberry Preserves

YIELD: 3 ½ CUPS

There are just enough tart blackberries in this preserve to highlight the blueberries' watery sweetness. With its low-key sugar and acid balance, Blueberry Blackberry Preserves flatters a wide variety of breads. How about trying it on Banana Bran Muffins or English Muffins with Yogurt (see Index)?

5 cups blueberries (1½ pounds)

2½ cups blackberries (12 ounces)

½ cup water

3 tablespoons fresh lemon juice, divided

2¼ cups sugar, divided

Pick over and rinse the blueberries and blackberries. Combine them with the water in a heavy, non-reactive 8-quart pot. Cover and bring to a simmer. Simmer, partially covered, for 10 minutes.

Strain off juices for 10 minutes and measure the quantity. Reserve the fruit pieces. Return juices to the pan, and reduce them to 2 cups if necessary. Add 2 tablespoons lemon juice to the simmering mixture, and begin adding 2 cups of sugar, ½ cup at a time, allowing the liquid to return to a boil each time before adding more. Continue cooking until it reaches the jell point, which is 8 degrees above the boiling point as measured on your thermometer. This will take 5 to 10 minutes.

Off heat, pour the hot jelly over the reserved fruits. Stir well and let the mixture steep for 15 minutes. Return fruit mixture to a clean pan. Add remaining lemon juice and return the preserves to a simmer. Slowly add another ¼ cup sugar. Boil until the thermometer reads 218° F., but cook no longer than 5 minutes. Stir regularly to keep the berries from sticking to the pan.

Pour the preserves into a 1-quart measure and let stand for 10 minutes, stirring occasionally to distribute the berries throughout. Fill hot, sterilized jars to within 1/4 inch of the rims. Wipe off the rims, attach new lids, and screw the caps on tightly. Invert jars briefly for a quick vacuum seal; or process in a boiling water bath, submerged by 1 inch, for 10 minutes.

Spicy Blueberry Preserves

Fresh, plump blueberries are so easy to eat out of hand or pop into muffin batter that their flavor potential is rarely developed beyond this point. But they can be rich, tart, and more intensely delicious when cooked in a preserve. The addition of spices further heightens the drama of their concentrated flavor.

This preserve is wonderful with warm Butter Pecan Muffins, Buckwheat Muffins, and Drop Scones (see Index). It also serves as a beautiful and tasty garnish in Blueberry Pecan Cheesecake (see Index). You will find it equally delicious when frozen in ice cream and sorbet or warmed in a sauce for baked stuffed peaches.

YIELD: 4 CUPS

> **3 pounds blueberries**
>
> **¹/₃ cup water**
>
> **1 4-inch cinnamon stick**
>
> **Bouquet Garni: 2 each: 2-inch strips fresh lemon peel, whole cloves, and allspice berries**
>
> **3 tablespoons fresh lemon juice, divided**
>
> **2¹/₄ cups sugar, divided**

Pick over, rinse, and drain the berries. Combine them with water in a heavy, non-reactive 8-quart pan. Add the cinnamon and the Bouquet Garni, tied with twine in a cheesecloth bag. Cover the pan and bring contents slowly to a simmer. Cook, partially covered, for 10 minutes.

Strain the blueberry juices for 5 minutes into a measuring container. Reserve the berries and spice bag in a large bowl. Pour the juices into a clean 5-quart pan and reduce them to 2 cups. Return juice to a boil, stir in 2 tablespoons lemon juice, and add 2 cups sugar, ¹/₂ cup at a time, allowing the mixture to return to a boil each time before adding more. Continue cooking until mixture reaches the jell point, which is 8 degrees above the boiling temperature as measured on your thermometer. This will take 5 to 10 minutes.

Pour the hot jelly into the bowl containing the reserved blueberries and spices. Let them steep together for 15 minutes. Return all to the pan and bring to a boil. Add remaining tablespoon of lemon juice and the last $\frac{1}{4}$ cup of sugar. Cook and stir frequently for 5 minutes; the thickened preserves should heat to 216–218° F.

Pour the finished preserves into a 1-quart measure and remove the spice bag. Stir the preserves once or twice over a 5-minute period. Fill hot, sterilized jars to within $\frac{1}{4}$ inch of the rims. Wipe the rims clean, attach new lids, and screw the caps on tightly. Invert the jars briefly for a quick vacuum seal, or process in a boiling water bath for 10 minutes, submerged by 1 inch.

Strawberry Preserves

What could be more gratifying than a thick layer of dark, sweet strawberry preserves on a warm Muffin or Cream Scone (see Index)? In fact, Strawberry Preserves complement all breads and double as a tasty sauce on fruit and ice cream.

YIELD: 4 CUPS

3 pounds strawberries (9 cups whole and cut berries)
1 cup water
3 tablespoons lemon juice, divided
2³/₄ cups sugar, divided

Rinse and hull the strawberries. Halve or quarter larger berries so all are of uniform size. Place berries and water in a heavy, non-reactive 8-quart pan. Cover and bring to a simmer, stirring occasionally to avoid sticking. Simmer, partially uncovered, for 10 minutes.

Strain the juice for 15 minutes. Reserve the berries in a large bowl. Place juice in a clean, deep 8-quart pan and reduce to 2¹/₂ cups. Skim foam off the juice, add 2 tablespoons lemon juice, and return to a boil. Stir in 2¹/₂ cups sugar, ¹/₂ cup at a time, allowing juice to return to a boil each time before adding more. Continue cooking until it reaches the jell point, which is 8 degrees above the boiling temperature as measured on your thermometer. This should happen in 5 to 10 minutes. Skim the jelly and pour over the reserved berries. Let them steep together for 15 minutes.

Return the preserves to the pan and bring to a boil. Stir in the remaining tablespoon of lemon juice and the remaining ¹/₄ cup of sugar. Boil for 5 minutes, stirring frequently to prevent sticking. The temperature should rise to 218° F. and the preserve thicken and sheet heavily from a metal spoon.

Skim the preserves and pour into a glass 1-quart measure. Allow the preserves to stand for 10 minutes, stirring occasionally to distribute the berries evenly throughout the preserve. Fill hot, sterilized jars to within ¹/₄ inch of the rims. Wipe the rims clean, attach new lids, and screw caps on tightly. Invert jars briefly for a quick vacuum seal, or process in a boiling water bath for 10 minutes, submerged by 1 inch.

Strawberry Blackberry Preserves

Why not save a jar of this preserve of succulent summer strawberries and blackberries for a late fall brunch buffet? Surround it with steamy fresh Buckwheat Muffins and textured Grape-Nuts® Muffins (see Index).

YIELD: 4 CUPS

2 pounds strawberries (6 cups, cut up)

1 pound fresh blackberries (4 cups)

¹/₂ cup water

4 tablespoons fresh lemon juice, divided

3¹/₃ cups sugar, divided

Rinse strawberries; hull and cut larger ones in half so they are all of uniform size. Combine them with blackberries and water in a heavy, non-reactive 5-quart pan. Cover and bring to a simmer. Simmer for 10 minutes, partially covered. Strain the berry juices for 15 minutes. Reserve the cooked berries in a bowl.

Return juice to the pan and reduce to 3 cups over high heat. Skim the fruit juice, add 2 tablespoons lemon juice, and return to a boil. Add 3 cups of sugar, ¹/₂ cup at a time, allowing the liquid to return to a boil each time before adding more. Continue boiling until mixture reaches the jell point, which is 8 degrees above the boiling point as measured on your thermometer. This should take 5 to 10 minutes.

Skim the jelly and stir in the reserved fruit pieces. Allow them to steep in the jelly for 15 minutes. Add remaining 2 tablespoons lemon juice and return the preserve to a boil. Add remaining ¹/₃ cup sugar and cook for 5 minutes, stirring frequently to prevent sticking. The temperature should rise to 216–218° F. and the preserve thicken and sheet heavily from a metal spoon.

Skim foam from the finished preserve and pour into a glass 1-quart measure. Let the preserve sit for 10 minutes, stirring occasionally to redistribute fruit pieces. Fill hot, sterilized jars to within $\frac{1}{4}$ inch of rims. Wipe the rims clean, attach new lids, and screw caps on tightly. Invert the jars briefly for a quick vacuum seal; or process 10 minutes in a boiling water bath, submerged by 1 inch.

Peach Preserves with Raspberries

Peaches with red raspberries is a combination made famous by Escoffier's Peche Melba, which is included in our dessert chapter. In fact, this preserve could make a wonderful Philadelphia–Style Ice Cream or soft–frozen sorbet (see Index), if you want to play up its dessert potential. But try it first as a spread on Cream Scones or Butter Pecan Muffins (see Index). These flavors are wonderful together at room temperature.

YIELD: 4 ½ CUPS

3 pounds peaches (7 cups peeled, pitted, chopped)

⅓ cup water

1 pound red raspberries (1 ½ pints)

3 tablespoons fresh lemon juice, divided

2 ⅓ cups sugar, divided

Dip the peaches in simmering water for 30 seconds. Submerge them immediately in ice water. When cool enough to handle, peel off the skins. Halve the peaches, remove pits, and chop into 1-inch dice. Pick over and rinse the raspberries.

Combine peaches with water in a deep, non-reactive 8-quart pan. Cover and bring to a boil. Simmer for 5 minutes partially covered. Add the raspberries, partially cover the pan, and continue cooking for 15 minutes. Uncover every 5 minutes to stir and check for sticking.

Strain the peach and raspberry juice for 15 minutes. Reserve the fruit in a large bowl. There will be about 3 cups of liquid. Reduce juice over high heat to 2 cups. Add 2 tablespoons lemon juice, and bring to a simmer. Add 2 cups sugar, ½ cup at a time, allowing mixture to return to a boil each time before adding more. Continue cooking until mixture reaches the jell point, which is 8 degrees above the boiling temperature as measured on your thermometer. This will take 5 to 10 minutes.

Pour the jelly over the reserved fruit pieces. Allow them to steep for 15 minutes. Return the preserves to a boil in a clean pan. Add the remaining tablespoon of lemon juice and bring preserves to a boil. Add the last ⅓ cup sugar and cook, stirring frequently, until the temperature reaches 215° F., but no longer than 5 minutes.

Fill hot, sterilized jars to within ¼ inch of the rims. Wipe the rims clean, attach new lids, and screw caps on tightly. Invert the jars briefly for a quick seal, or process them in a boiling water bath, submerged by 1 inch, for 10 minutes.

Italian Plum Preserves

The soft flesh of Italian plums has a sweet, rather nondescript taste. The tart and fragrant flavor that lies in its thin, dark skin is developed in this recipe. Zucchini Bread and Oatmeal Muffins (see Index) are my favorite bread partners for this preserve.

YIELD: 4 CUPS

3 pounds Italian plums, pitted and quartered

1 cup water

2 tablespoons fresh lemon juice, divided

2 cups sugar plus 2 tablespoons

Combine plum pieces with water in a heavy, non-reactive 5-quart pan. Cover the pan and bring liquid to a boil; uncover and simmer steadily for 20 minutes.

Strain juices for 30 minutes. Reserve the plum pieces. Reduce juices to 2 cups, add 1 tablespoon lemon juice, and begin adding the 2 cups of sugar, ½ cup at a time, allowing the mixture to return to a boil each time before adding more. Continue cooking until the liquid reaches the jell point, which is 8 degrees above the boiling point as measured on your thermometer. This should take 5 to 10 minutes.

Off heat, stir the plum quarters into the hot jelly and steep for 15 minutes.

Return preserves to a boil. Stir in remaining tablespoon of lemon juice and 2 tablespoons of sugar. Boil for 10 minutes, stirring frequently to avoid sticking as the liquids reduce and the temperature rises to 218° F.

Off heat, skim off foam and fill hot, sterilized jars to within ¼ inch of the rims. Wipe the rims clean, attach new lids, and screw the caps on tightly. Invert the jars briefly for a quick vacuum seal, or process in a boiling water bath, submerged by 1 inch, for 10 minutes.

Four-Berry Preserves

Thanks to commercial growers, we now can purchase all these berries at peak ripeness at the same time in June and July. This preserve is so rich in aroma and flavor that a warm, chewy Muffin of any kind (see Index) would be a welcome partner.

YIELD: 3 ½ CUPS

16 ounces strawberries

12 ounces blueberries

7 ounces blackberries

4 ounces red raspberries

½ cup water

3 tablespoons fresh lemon juice, divided

1½ cups sugar plus 2 tablespoons

Rinse, drain, hull, and halve the strawberries. Rinse and drain remaining berries. Combine all four berry varieties with water in a heavy 8-quart pan. Cover the pan and bring to a simmer. Uncover and simmer for 10 minutes. Strain juices for 15 minutes. Reserve the berries in a large mixing bowl.

Reduce the strained juices to 1 ½ cups. Add 2 tablespoons lemon juice and return to a boil. Add 1 ½ cups sugar, ½ cup at a time, allowing the mixture to return to a boil each time before adding more. Continue cooking until mixture reaches the jell point, which is 8 degrees above the boiling temperature as measured on your thermometer. This should take 5 to 10 minutes.

Off heat, pour jelly over the fruit pieces and let them steep for 15 minutes. Return the preserves to a clean 8-quart pan. Add remaining lemon juice and return to a boil. Stir in the remaining 2 tablespoons sugar and simmer 5 minutes, stirring frequently to prevent sticking.

Pour the hot preserve into a 1-quart glass measure. Let it sit for 5 minutes, stirring occasionally. Fill hot, sterilized jars to within $\frac{1}{4}$ inch of the rims. Wipe the rims clean, attach new lids, and screw caps on tightly. Invert jars briefly for a quick vacuum seal, or process in a boiling water bath, submerged by 1 inch, for 10 minutes.

Blackberry Ginger Preserves

The dark, toothsome blackberry makes a spectacular preserve, full of sweet-sour contrast and the fragrance of wilderness. I have added ginger's warm sensations and spicy aroma for emphasis. Blackberries and buckwheat are a favorite combination of mine. You could enjoy this preserve with either the blini or muffin recipe (see Index). If you like the meaty pulp of this berry and its crunchy seeds, spread it on English Muffins (see Index) and enjoy a delicious chewing experience. This preserve will also appear again as a sauce for fresh pears.

YIELD: 4 CUPS

3 pounds blackberries

$^1/_2$ cup water

2 slices fresh ginger (each the size of a quarter)

3 tablespoons lemon juice, divided

2 cups sugar plus 2 tablespoons

Rinse and drain the berries. Combine with water in a heavy, non-reactive 8-quart pan. Cover and bring to a simmer. Uncover and simmer the berries for 10 minutes. Strain the juices for 15 minutes. Reserve the blackberries in a large mixing bowl.

Measure the blackberry juice and reduce it to 2 cups. Bring the juice to a boil with the gingerroot slices and 2 tablespoons lemon juice. Stir in 2 cups sugar, $^1/_2$ cup at a time, allowing the pan to return to a boil between additions. Continue to boil until mixture reaches the jell point, which is 8 degrees above the boiling temperature as measured on your thermometer. This will take about 5 minutes.

Pour the jelly over the reserved berries and allow preserve to steep for 15 minutes. Return the preserve to a clean pan, add remaining tablespoon of lemon juice, cover, and bring to a boil. Add the remaining sugar and cook to the jell point, another 5 minutes or so.

Pour the hot preserves into a 2-quart measure. Remove the gingerroot slices. Let the preserve sit for 5 minutes, stirring occasionally.

Pour preserves into hot, sterilized jars to within $1/4$ inch of the rims. Wipe the rims clean, attach new lids, and screw caps on tightly. Invert the jars briefly to create a quick vacuum seal; or process in a boiling water bath, submerged by 1 inch, for 10 minutes.

Red Raspberry Preserves

These preserves enhance any breakfast, served on an English Muffin (see Index), and can be very dressy for high tea with Cream Scones and Butter Pecan Muffins (see Index). A look through Chapter 9 will show you how many delicious dessert alliances can be made with these preserves. This recipe is the star of the Linzer Torte and the fillip of the Peach Melba (see Index).

YIELD: 5 CUPS

3 pounds red raspberries (9 cups)

$^1/_2$ cup water

3 tablespoons lemon juice, divided

2 cups sugar plus 2 tablespoons

Rinse and drain the berries. Combine with water in a heavy, non-reactive 8-quart pan. Cover and bring to a simmer. Uncover and simmer the berries for 10 minutes. Strain the juices for 15 minutes. Reserve the berries in a large mixing bowl. Measure raspberry juice and reduce it to 2 cups.

Bring juice to a boil, stir in 2 tablespoons lemon juice, and begin adding the 2 cups of sugar $\frac{1}{2}$ cup at a time, allowing the mixture to return to a boil each time before adding more. Cook until the mixture reaches the jell point, which is 8 degrees above the boiling temperature as measured on your thermometer. This will take less than 5 minutes.

Stir the hot jelly into the reserved raspberries and let them steep for 15 minutes. Return to a boil. Add remaining tablespoon of lemon juice and 2 tablespoons sugar. Continue cooking until preserve reaches the jell point. This should take 7 to 10 minutes. Boil for an additional minute. Stir frequently during this time to prevent sticking.

Pour the preserves into a 2-quart measure. Hold for 5 minutes, stirring occasionally. Skim preserves and fill hot, sterilized jars to within $\frac{1}{4}$ inch of rims. Wipe the rims clean, attach new lids, and screw the caps on tightly. Invert jars briefly for a quick vacuum seal; or submerge them by 1 inch in a boiling water bath for 10 minutes.

Raspberry Red Currant Preserves

The proliferation of farmers' markets has brought the red currant into greater circulation in late June and July. It's worthwhile seeking them out. Their tartness is a wonderful complement to other berries. This jam is delicious with all the breads. My favorites are the Buttermilk Currant Scones and Tea Brack (see Index).

YIELD: 5 CUPS

> 2 **cups red currant juice (strained from 2$^1/_2$ pounds red currants)**
> 2 **pounds red raspberries**
> 3 **tablespoons lemon juice, divided**
> 3$^1/_4$ **cups sugar, divided**

Follow directions in Master Recipe for Red Currant Jelly (see page 101) to extract juice from the currants.

Combine raspberries and currant juice in an 8-quart pan, cover, and bring to a boil. Uncover and simmer for 10 minutes. Strain the juices for 15 minutes. Reserve the berries in the sieve. Measure the juice and either reduce or add water to measure 3 cups.

Add 2 tablespoons lemon juice to the strained fruit juices in a clean 8-quart pan. Cover and bring to a boil. Uncover and add 3 cups sugar, $^1/_2$ cup at a time, allowing the liquid to regain a boil each time before adding more. Cook mixture to the jell point, which is 8 degrees above the boiling temperature as measured on your thermometer. This will happen within 5 minutes.

Stir the reserved berries into the hot jelly and steep for 15 minutes. Add remaining tablespoon of lemon juice. Cover the pan and bring to a boil. Uncover and stir in remaining $^1/_4$ cup sugar. Keep at a boil until the jell temperature is reached, about 5 minutes.

Pour the preserves into a 2-quart glass measure. Let the preserves sit for 5 minutes, stirring occasionally to redistribute the berries. Fill hot, sterilized jars to within $^1/_4$ inch of rims. Wipe the rims clean, attach new lids, and screw caps on tightly. Invert jars briefly for a quick seal; or process in a boiling water bath, submerged by 1 inch, for 10 minutes.

Blueberry Raspberry Preserves

This preserve of blueberries and raspberries is a special midsummer treat to serve with warm muffins or scones (see Index for recipes).

YIELD: 5 ½ CUPS

- **2 pounds fresh blueberries (6 cups)**
- **1 pound red raspberries**
- **½ cup water**
- **3 tablespoons fresh lemon juice, divided**
- **3¼ cups sugar, divided**

Rinse and pick over the berries. Combine with water in a heavy, non-reactive 8-quart pan. Cover and bring to a boil. Uncover and simmer for 10 minutes. Strain juice for 15 minutes. Reserve the berries in a large bowl. Measure the juice and either reduce or add water to measure 3 cups.

Bring juice to a simmer in a clean 8-quart pan. Stir in 2 tablespoons lemon juice and add 3 cups sugar, ½ cup at a time, allowing the mixture to return to a boil each time before adding more. Boil mixture until it reaches the jell point, which is 8 degrees above the boiling temperature as measured on your thermometer. This will take place within 5 minutes.

Stir the hot jelly into the reserved berries and let them steep for 15 minutes. Return to a clean pan, add remaining tablespoon of lemon juice, and return preserves to a boil. Stir in the remaining sugar and boil until the thermometer reads 218° F. but no longer than 10 more minutes, stirring frequently.

Off heat, fill hot, sterilized jars to within ¼ inch of the rims. Wipe the rims clean, attach new lids, and screw caps on tightly. Invert jars briefly for a quick seal; or process in a boiling water bath, submerged by 1 inch, for 10 minutes.

Apple Red Raspberry Preserves

This pair of fruits produces a preserve of tart flavor, floral aroma, and great pectin strength. They cook into a lovely crimson mixture of tiny seeds, soft pulp, and firm apple slices.

Serve this luscious preserve on Apple Cinnamon Muffins, Grape–Nuts® Muffins, or Cream Scones (see Index). It will also perform beautifully as a sauce on French Toast or when frozen in a sorbet.

YIELD: 5 ½ CUPS

> **2 pounds firm, tart apples (Granny Smith, Jonathan, or Cortland)**
>
> **1 ½ pounds red raspberries**
>
> **½ cup water**
>
> **3 tablespoons lemon juice, divided**
>
> **2 ¾ cups sugar, divided**

Peel, quarter, core, and thinly slice the apples. Combine apple pieces with raspberries and water in a heavy, non-reactive 5-quart pan. Cover and bring to a boil. Uncover and simmer for 10 minutes. Stir occasionally to prevent sticking.

Strain the hot juices from the fruit pieces for 15 minutes. Reserve the fruit pieces in a large bowl. Juices should measure 2 ½ cups. Add water if there is less or reduce to that amount over high heat if there is more.

Bring fruit juice to a boil and add 2 tablespoons lemon juice and 2 ½ cups of sugar, ½ cup at a time, waiting for the liquid to return to a boil each time before adding more. Continue boiling to the jell point, which is 8 degrees above the boiling temperature as measured on your thermometer. This should take about 5 minutes.

Off heat, stir jelly into the fruit pieces. Let them steep for 15 minutes. Return the preserves to a boil in a clean pan, and add remaining tablespoon of lemon juice and final $\frac{1}{4}$ cup sugar. Cook for 5 minutes, stirring quite often to prevent sticking. The mixture will be quite thick, and its temperature should rise to 216° F.

Transfer the preserve into a 2-quart measure and allow it to sit for 5 minutes, stirring occasionally. Pour the preserve into hot, sterilized jars to within $\frac{1}{4}$ inch of the rims. Wipe the rims clean, attach new lids, and screw caps on tightly. Invert jars briefly for a quick vacuum seal; or process in a boiling water bath, submerged by 1 inch, for 10 minutes.

Pear and Grape Preserves

Pears and grapes can be cooked into the sweet preserves that result from this recipe or into a no-sugar jam (see Index). Savor this pear and grape combination on Oatmeal Muffins, Butter Pecan Muffins, or Drop Scones (see Index).

YIELD: 4 ½ CUPS

3 pounds Concord grapes (3 cups strained juice)

1 cup water

3 pounds ripe Bartlett pears

3 tablespoons lemon juice, divided

3 ⅓ cups sugar, divided

Rinse and stem the grapes. Bring them to a simmer with 1 cup water in a heavy, non-reactive 4-quart pan. Cover the pan and simmer slowly for 30 minutes. Lift the cover regularly to stir and crush the grapes against the side of the pan.

Strain grape juice for 2 hours through a sieve lined with cheesecloth. You should have about 3 cups of juice. If there is less, add water to make up the difference. If there is more, reduce juice to 3 cups. Discard grapes.

Peel, quarter, and core the pears. Thinly slice the pears and combine them in an 8-quart pan with the grape juice and 2 tablespoons lemon juice. Bring mixture to a boil, regulate heat to a gentle simmer, cover, and cook for 10 minutes.

Off heat, strain the juice for 15 minutes. Reserve pear pieces in a large mixing bowl. Reduce the juice to 3 cups.

Bring juice to a boil and add 3 cups of sugar, ½ cup at a time, allowing the liquid to return to a boil between additions. Continue boiling until mixture reaches the jell point, which is 8 degrees above the boiling point as measured on your thermometer. This should take 5 to 7 minutes.

Off heat, stir the jelly into the pear pieces and steep for 15 minutes. Return the preserve to a boil, add remaining tablespoon of lemon juice, and gradually stir in the remaining sugar. Boil until the preserve sheets from a spoon, but no longer than 10 minutes. Stir quite frequently to prevent sticking.

Off heat, skim the surface and pour preserves into hot, sterilized jars to within $1/4$ inch of the rims. Wipe the rims clean, attach new lids, and screw caps on tightly. Invert the jars briefly for a quick vacuum seal; or process in a boiling water bath, submerged by 1 inch, for 10 minutes

Apple Grape Preserves

The rich scent of apples and grapes sitting in the warm September sun at roadside stands recalls pleasant memories of an early fall harvest. Now you can capture this evocative fragrance in a preserve to enjoy throughout the winter. Apple Grape Preserves taste wonderful served with freshly baked Apple Cinnamon Muffins (see Index).

YIELD: 4 CUPS

> **3 pounds Concord grapes (3 cups strained juice)**
>
> **¹/₂ cup water**
>
> **2 cups Granny Smith *or* Golden Delicious apples**
>
> **3 tablespoons lemon juice, divided**
>
> **Sugar, divided**

Rinse and remove grapes from their stems. Combine water with grapes in a heavy, non-reactive 8-quart pan, cover, and bring to a boil. Uncover, reduce the heat to a simmer, and cook 10 minutes. Strain grape juice for 2 hours. Reduce it to 3 cups if necessary. Discard the grapes.

Peel, quarter, and core the apples. Slice them into narrow wedges. Combine the apple pieces with the grape juice and 2 tablespoons lemon juice in a 5-quart pan. Cover the pan and bring to a boil. Uncover and simmer for 10 minutes. Apples will soften but remain whole. Strain juice for 15 minutes. Reserve the apples in a large mixing bowl.

Measure strained juice and set aside an equal volume of sugar. Bring juice to a boil and add sugar, ½ cup at a time, allowing juice to return to a boil each time before adding more. Continue cooking over high heat until the mixture reaches the jell point, which is 8 degrees above the boiling point as measured on your thermometer. This should take less than 5 minutes.

Remove the juice from the heat, pour it over the apple pieces, and let steep for 15 minutes. Return the preserves to a boil in a clean pan. Stir in the last tablespoon of lemon juice and an additional ⅓ cup of sugar. Let the mixture cook at a boil until it reaches 218° F. but no longer than 10 minutes. The preserve will be thick and sheet from a spoon. Stir the pan frequently to prevent sticking.

Off heat, skim foam from the preserve. Fill hot, sterilized jars to within ¼ inch of the rims. Wipe the rims clean, attach new lids, and screw caps on tightly. Invert the jars briefly for a quick vacuum seal; or process in a boiling water bath, submerged by 1 inch, for 10 minutes.

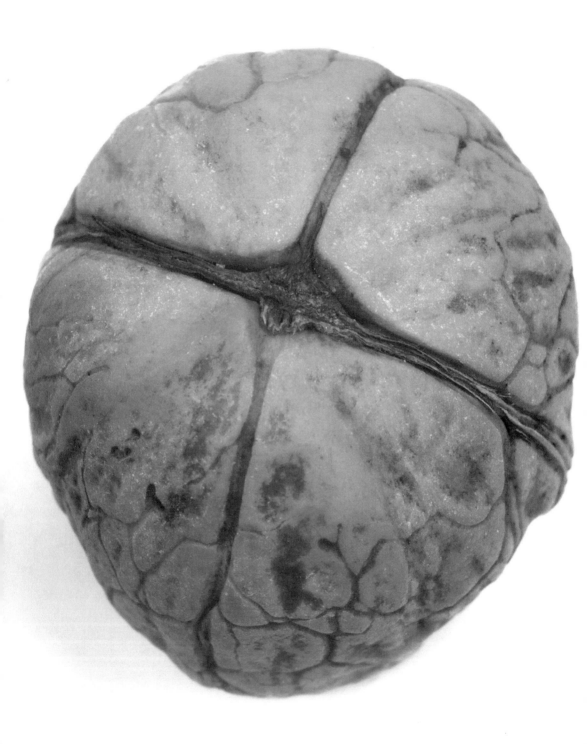

8
BREADS AND MUFFINS

Sit down to a restaurant breakfast anywhere in America, and you're likely to be served dry toast or a muffin with preserves portioned in tiny plastic cups. What a difference it makes to have your own homemade bread and jam sitting before you first thing in the morning. It's worth getting out of bed for. Served with a cup of hot tea or dark-roast coffee and the morning papers, freshly warm bread and jam is an essential daily ritual.

The baking powder breads and muffins in this chapter are easy enough to make in the morning even before you've had a cup of coffee. If you're not up to rising and baking early, plan ahead and defrost some you've already made beforehand. This routine will come easily once you learn to always be thinking ahead to your next meal.

English Muffins, French Toast, and the Giant Sunday Popover are bigger projects, more suited to the slower pace of weekend breakfasts. They are also perfect entertaining foods, say, at a brunch for friends. That would be a good opportunity to bring out Risen Biscuits and Blinis, too. Once the preserves are gone, you can serve the breads with ham and smoked salmon from the buffet.

It's one thing to enjoy a fruit preserve as a condiment and quite another to sit down and devour an entire jar-full in one sitting. If my reading of the *Decameron* is correct, the elegant Florentine youths of Boccaccio's day spooned rich preserves directly onto their pampered palates. Three centuries later and farther north, published diagrams of table settings in fashionable 17th-century English households displayed molded jellies on elaborate dessert tables. Although shapely and sensuous when presented in such regal settings, we would find these molded fruit preserves cloying to the point of palate numbing today.

One final tip for securing the tastiest companions for homemade jams and jellies: toast or reheat the bread before serving.
This goes for store-bought, even day-old, bread as well. You
can revive bread by placing it in a 300 degree F. oven for 10
minutes. The aroma of warm bread has such universal appeal
that if you weren't hungry before, you will be when it arrives
at the table.

BASIC BAKING INGREDIENTS AND PROCEDURES

A few basic rules apply to all these bread recipes despite their
technical differences.

- Large eggs and unsalted butter are standard ingredients in
  all these recipes.
- Purchase fresh flours if your supplies have been stored for
  more than 4 months at room temperature or more than
  6 months refrigerated or frozen.
- Unless otherwise specified, begin with all ingredients at
  room temperature.
- Measure dry ingredients in metal cups, fill with a scoop,
  and scrape flat without compressing.
- Measure liquids in heatproof glass measuring containers.
- Place a mercury oven thermometer in your oven to verify
  its temperature before baking. Ovens vary from calibrated
  settings over time and need to be checked with a thermometer periodically or recalibrated every few months.
- Test breads and muffins with an instant-read thermometer
  to assure that they are done. A reading of 200 degrees F.
  assures that the wheat starch has gelatinized.

BASIC TECHNIQUES

- The techniques for assembling ingredients are designed
  either to inhibit or to expand the gluten strength of the
  wheat flour, depending on the bread texture desired.
- In the baking powder bread recipes for muffins, zucchini
  bread, tea brack, popovers, and scones, dry ingredients
  are gently worked into the wet ingredients. The dough or
  batter is stirred until the ingredients are just blended.

184

Additional mixing will only tighten the flour's gluten muscle. If any of your baking powder breads rise to a jutting peak rather than a soft mound shape, you have overbeaten the batter.

· In the yeast breads, gluten activity is encouraged by pulling and stretching the dough. This kneading activity gives the English Muffins and Risen Biscuits (see pages 210–214) a firm, chewy texture. However, the yeast in the Russian Buckwheat Blinis with Blackberry Sauce (see page 206) is used only to flavor the dough, so no kneading activity is called for.

· Butter and oil used to prepare baking molds and pans are not listed as ingredients.

Butter Pecan Muffins

Usually all one needs to enjoy the rich flavor of steamy, warm pecan muffins is the muffin itself. But by the time a second muffin is on your plate, so is a mild Orange Marmalade and a tablespoon of Blueberry Preserves (see Index). In this case, more is better.

YIELD: 12 MUFFINS

3/4 **cup chopped pecans**

6 **tablespoons unsalted butter**

3 **tablespoons brown sugar**

4 **teaspoons baking powder**

2 **cups unbleached flour**

1/2 **teaspoon salt**

1 **cup milk**

4 **large eggs**

Preheat the oven to 350° F. and toast the pecan pieces for 10 minutes. Butter a pan that holds 12 muffins. Melt 6 tablespoons of butter and reserve it. Raise the oven setting to 400°.

Measure the sugar, baking powder, flour, and salt into a 2-quart bowl and stir well. Make a well in the center and pour in the melted butter, milk, and eggs. Beat the wet ingredients together and gradually incorporate the dry ingredients. Stir together until just blended.

Fold the warm pecans into the batter.

Spoon the batter into the molds and bake for 20 minutes or until the muffins are puffed, lightly browned, and register 200° F. internally on an instant-read thermometer. Let them cool in the pan for 5 minutes. Unmold and serve warm with jam or preserves.

Cornmeal Muffins

Here is a muffin recipe that can be modified for almost any occasion. Made as given below, the muffins can be served at a meal or tea with delicate Lime Marmalade or Peach Blueberry Jam (see Index). If you were to substitute brown sugar for white, bacon drippings for butter, a coarsely ground cornmeal, and buttermilk for milk, you would have a Country-Style Cornmeal Muffin (see below). This would call for a jar of zesty Apricot Orange Jam or Damson Plum Jam (see Index).

YIELD: 12 MUFFINS

> 2 tablespoons sugar
>
> 3 tablespoons unsalted butter at room temperature
>
> $3/4$ cup cornmeal
>
> 4 large eggs
>
> 1 cup milk
>
> 1 cup unbleached flour
>
> 1 tablespoon baking powder
>
> $1/2$ teaspoon salt
>
> $1/4$ teaspoon freshly ground black pepper

Preheat the oven to 400° F. Butter a pan that holds 12 muffins. Cream the sugar with the butter in a 2-quart bowl. Stir in the cornmeal, eggs (1 at a time), and milk.

Measure flour, baking powder, salt, and pepper into a 1-quart bowl and mix well. Pour the dry mixture over the wet and stir together until just blended.

Ladle the batter into the molds and bake for 20 minutes until the muffins are puffed, golden brown, and register 200° F. internally on an instant-read thermometer. Let them cool in the pan for 5 minutes. Unmold the muffins and serve them warm with jam or preserves.

Country-Style Cornmeal Muffins

    2 tablespoons brown sugar

    3 tablespoons bacon drippings

 $^3/_4$ cup coarse cornmeal

    4 large eggs

    1 cup buttermilk

    1 cup unbleached white flour

    2 teaspoons baking powder

    1 teaspoon baking soda

 $^1/_2$ teaspoon salt

 $^1/_4$ teaspoon freshly ground black pepper

Follow the directions for the Cornmeal Muffins above.

Oatmeal Muffins

Sometimes you want a bread that will showcase your preserving prowess. An oatmeal muffin offers just the right profile, with its slightly chewy texture and warm, fresh grain scent. Now is your chance to serve that fabulous Black Raspberry Cassis Jam or the exotic Kiwifruit Mint Jam (see Index) and really wow your guests.

YIELD: 12 MUFFINS

- 1 **cup instant oatmeal**
- 1 **cup milk**
- 2 **tablespoons unsalted butter**
- 3 **tablespoons brown sugar**
- 1½ **cups unbleached flour**
- 4 **teaspoons baking powder**
- ½ **teaspoon salt**
- 4 **large eggs**

Preheat the oven to 400° F. Butter a pan that holds 12 muffins.

Measure the oatmeal into a 2-quart bowl. Heat the milk and butter to a simmer. Pour this hot mixture over the oatmeal and let it stand for 10 minutes.

Measure and mix together the sugar, flour, baking powder, and salt in a 1-quart bowl. Beat the eggs into the oatmeal mixture. Pour the dry mixture over the wet, and stir until just blended.

Ladle the batter into the molds and bake for 15 minutes or until the muffins are puffed, browned, and register 200° F. internally on an instant-read thermometer. Let them cool in the pan for 5 minutes. Unmold and eat warm with jam or marmalade.

Apple Cinnamon Muffins

This muffin can easily become the delicious byproduct of a Pectin Stock recipe. Simply press the strained apple pieces through a food mill, and fold the applesauce into the other muffin ingredients. The soft apple pulp gives the bread a moist, delicate texture and cinnamon revives the apple's floral scent. One of the snappy no-sugar jams would taste good with this subtle muffin. My choice would be the No-Sugar Apple Blackberry Jam or No-Sugar Pear and Blueberry Jam (see Index).

YIELD: 12 MUFFINS

- **3 tablespoons soft unsalted butter**
- **2 tablespoons brown sugar**
- **3 large eggs**
- **1 cup unsweetened applesauce *or* apple puree (*see* Apple Pectin Stock, p. 103)**
- **1¹/₂ cups unbleached flour**
- **¹/₂ teaspoon ground cinnamon**
- **¹/₂ teaspoon salt**
- **4 teaspoons baking powder**

Preheat oven to 400° F. Butter a pan that holds 12 muffins.

Cream the butter with the brown sugar in a 2-quart bowl. Add eggs 1 at a time, mixing each in well. Stir in the applesauce.

Measure the flour, cinnamon, salt, and baking powder into a 1-quart bowl and stir together. Pour dry mixture over the wet, and stir together until they are just blended. Spoon the batter into the molds and bake for 15 minutes or until muffins are puffed, browned, and register 200° F. internally on an instant-read thermometer. Let them cool in the pan for 5 minutes. Unmold and serve muffins warm with butter and marmalade.

Buckwheat Muffins

Watch this muffin raise eyebrows in delight at its gutsy array of scents and flavors. The buckwheat flour has a bitter tang; the buttermilk is pleasingly sour. Serve an assertive fruit flavor preserve that can hold its own with this robust partner: Plum Jam with Cardamom, Orange Cranberry Marmalade, or Pineapple Lemon Preserves (see Index).

YIELD: 12 MUFFINS

4 tablespoons butter, melted

¹/₂ cup buckwheat flour

1 cup unbleached flour

2 teaspoons baking powder

1 teaspoon baking soda

¹/₂ teaspoon salt

1 cup buttermilk

4 large eggs

2 tablespoons maple syrup

Preheat the oven to 400° F. Butter a pan that holds 12 muffins. Melt the butter and reserve.

Combine and blend together the buckwheat flour, unbleached flour, baking powder, baking soda, and salt in a mixing bowl. Make a well in the center. Pour the buttermilk, eggs, and maple syrup into the well. Mix the wet ingredients together with a fork. Gradually stir them into the dry ingredients with a spatula. When they are just mixed, fold in the melted butter.

Spoon the batter into the molds and bake for 15 minutes or until the muffins are puffed, browned, and register 200° F. internally on an instant-read thermometer. Let them cool in the pan for 5 minutes. Unmold and serve muffins warm with butter and jam.

Grape-Nuts® Muffins

In this recipe the rich wheat and malted barley aroma of Grape-Nuts® is magnified by cooking, and its famous gravel-crunch texture is softened to flavorful rubble. Try this muffin with the delicate Blueberry Jam with Mint or the sweet, hot Apple Ginger Jam (see Index).

YIELD: 12 MUFFINS

1 cup Grape-Nuts® cereal

1 cup buttermilk

4 tablespoons unsalted butter, melted

4 eggs, lightly beaten

1 cup unbleached flour

2 teaspoons baking powder

1 teaspoon baking soda

2 tablespoons sugar

1/2 teaspoon salt

Preheat the oven to 400° F. Butter a pan that holds 12 muffins.

Combine Grape-Nuts®, buttermilk, melted butter, and eggs in a 2-quart bowl; stir and let stand 10 minutes. Measure flour, baking powder, baking soda, sugar, and salt into a 1-quart bowl and stir well. Pour dry mixture over the wet and stir together until just blended.

Ladle the batter into the molds and bake for 15 minutes or until muffins are puffed, lightly browned, and register 200° F. internally on an instant-read thermometer. Let them cool in the pan for 5 minutes. Unmold and serve muffins warm with sweet butter and jam.

Banana Bran Muffins

This muffin pairs soft, sweet bananas with the textured whole-grain flavors of wheat and bran. A colorful, acidic preserve such as Kiwifruit Pineapple Jam or Nectarine Orange Jam (see Index) makes a tasty partner. You could also serve it with a zucchini or pepper marmalade and enjoy the composition of a vegetable preserve on dark bread.

YIELD: 12 MUFFINS

$^2/_3$ cup wheat bran

1 cup whole-wheat flour

$^2/_3$ cup unbleached flour

$^1/_4$ cup brown sugar

$^1/_2$ teaspoon salt

4 teaspoons baking powder

4 tablespoons unsalted butter, melted

$^1/_2$ cup milk

4 large eggs

2 large bananas, mashed (1 cup)

Preheat oven to 400° F. Butter a pan that holds 12 muffins.

Combine the bran, flours, sugar, salt, and baking powder in a mixing bowl. Blend these ingredients together and make a well in the center. Stir melted butter, milk, and eggs together in a 2-cup measure. Pour the wet ingredients and the banana mash into the well of the dry mixture. Fold together until just blended.

Ladle the batter into the molds and bake for 20 minutes or until the muffins are puffed, brown, and register 200° F. internally on an instant-read thermometer. Let them cool in the pan for 5 minutes. Unmold and enjoy warm muffins with jam or marmalade.

Marmalade Muffins

YIELD: 12 MUFFINS

    2 **cups unbleached flour**

$^1/_2$ **cup sugar**

    1 **tablespoon baking powder**

$^1/_2$ **teaspoon sea salt**

    1 **cup milk**

    6 **tablespoons unsalted butter, melted**

    2 **large eggs**

    1 **teaspoon vanilla extract**

$^1/_4$ **teaspoon almond extract**

$^1/_4$ **cup orange marmalade**

$^1/_2$ **cup slivered almonds**

    Confectioners' sugar

Preheat oven to 400° F. Butter or spray a 12-muffin mold.

Combine and stir to blend the flour, sugar, baking powder, and salt in a large mixing bowl. Make a well in the center. Stir together the milk, butter, eggs, and extracts. Pour the liquid into the well, and stir together until just blended.

Fill the muffin molds half full with batter. Spoon a teaspoon of marmalade into the center of each mold. Top with the remaining batter. Scatter on the almond slivers.

Bake for 20 minutes or until the muffins are golden and register 200° F. internally on an instant-read thermometer. Cool muffins on a rack. Sprinkle on confectioners' sugar before serving.

Zucchini Bread

This is one of my favorite summer breads. I never tire of making substitutions and variations in the recipe. But I always serve it the same way. Slices are cut thin. One side is slathered with fresh cream cheese, the other with Red Currant Jelly or an equally tangy Cherry Red Raspberry Jam (see Index). The sandwiches are cut diagonally into triangles and served with a cup of hot tea.

YIELD: 1 LARGE LOAF OR 18 MUFFINS

     2 **cups grated zucchini**

     2 **cups whole-wheat flour**

     1 **cup unbleached white flour**

     1 **cup sugar**

     1 **teaspoon salt**

     1 **teaspoon baking powder**

     1 **teaspoon baking soda**

$^1/_4$ **teaspoon each: mace. cinnamon, ginger, cardamom**

     3 **large eggs**

     1 **cup salad oil**

     2 **teaspoons vanilla**

        Grated peel of 1 lemon (optional)

     1 **cup currants, chopped dried apricots and dates,** *or* **chopped nuts (optional)**

Preheat oven to 325° F. Lightly oil a 9x5-inch loaf pan or a muffin pan that has 18 molds.

Grate the zucchini and reserve. Combine flours, sugar, salt, baking powder, baking soda, and spices in a 2-quart bowl and stir to mix well. Add the eggs to the salad oil in a 2-cup measure and beat lightly. Stir in the vanilla.

195

Make a well in the center of the dry ingredients, pour in the wet ones, and stir from the center, slowly incorporating the dry into the wet ingredients. Mix only until a batter forms.

Fold in the zucchini along with optional lemon peel, dried fruits, or nuts and ladle the mixture into the pan or muffin molds.

Bake for 1 hour or until an instant thermometer inserted in the center of the loaf reaches 200° F. Allow the loaf to cool for 10 minutes in the pan (5 minutes for the muffins) before unmolding. Serve bread at room temperature (serve muffins warm) with an invigorating sweet-tart jelly.

Tea Brack

This recipe first intrigued me because tea was an ingredient. I was delighted to find that the tea offered a slightly astringent counterpoint to the otherwise predominantly sweet ingredients. Tea Brack also has an attractively firm texture dotted with chewy sweet bits and crunchy nuts. I prefer to serve it with a lively sweet-sour jelly such as Grape, Cinnamon Cranberry Apple, or Chardonnay (see Index).

YIELD: 1 LARGE LOAF, ABOUT 2 DOZEN SLICES

$3/4$ **cup white raisins**

$3/4$ **cup dried currants**

$1^1/4$ **cups light brown sugar, firmly packed**

$1^1/2$ **cups cold black tea**

2 **cups unbleached white flour**

$1^1/2$ **teaspoons baking powder**

$1/2$ **teaspoon each: cinnamon and nutmeg**

$1/4$ **teaspoon salt**

$1/2$ **cup crushed walnuts**

1 **large egg**

$1/4$ **cup salad oil**

Combine raisins, currants, brown sugar, and tea in a mixing bowl. Cover and let stand overnight.

Preheat oven to 325° F. and generously oil a 9x5-inch loaf pan.

Blend flour, baking powder, spices, and salt in a large bowl. Crush the walnut pieces to the size of peas and toss them into the dry ingredients.

Make a well in the dry mixture. Add the beaten egg and oil along with the fruits and tea mixture. Stir from the center, gradually adding the wet to the dry ingredients to make a smooth batter.

Pour batter into the prepared pan and bake for 1 ½ hours or until an instant thermometer inserted in the center of the loaf reaches 200° F.

Let the loaf cool in the pan for 30 minutes. Loosen the sides and invert to release the bread. Cool to room temperature before serving.

Cream Scones

This recipe produces a butter-fragrant and tender biscuit. Dress it with a truly fancy topping like Red Raspberry Preserves (see Index). The preserves with liqueurs— Nectarine Jam with Grand Marnier and Pear Preserves with Pernod (see Index)— are also good here.

YIELD: 16 SCONES

$2^{1}/_{2}$ **cups cake flour**

$^{1}/_{4}$ **cup sugar**

4 **teaspoons baking powder**

1 **teaspoon salt**

6 **tablespoons cold unsalted butter**

$^{2}/_{3}$ **cup light cream**

1 **egg beaten with 1 tablespoon cream**

Preheat oven to 375° F. Butter and flour a large baking sheet.

Combine flour, sugar, baking powder, and salt in a 2-quart bowl and stir to mix. Cut the cold butter into 24 small pieces (quarter it lengthwise and cut each quarter crosswise into 6 pieces) and work it into the dry ingredients with fingertips or a pastry blender until the texture is mealy. Stir in cream until a ball forms. (If using a food processor, it will take 6 to 8 rapid on-and-off motions to pulverize the butter into the dry ingredients. Then add the cream and run the machine until a ball is barely formed.)

Roll the dough out ½ inch thick on a lightly floured work surface. Cut into 2½-inch biscuits with a cutter or the rim of a glass. Brush tops lightly with egg wash and bake for 15 minutes or until the scones are puffed and lightly browned. Cool them briefly and serve warm with jam or marmalade and Crème Fraîche (see Index).

Buttermilk Currant Scones

YIELD: 18, 2-INCH SCONES

Substitute for light cream:

$^1/_2$ teaspoon baking soda

$^2/_3$ cup buttermilk

Add:

$^1/_2$ cup currants

Follow directions for Cream Scones, above, with these modifications: Stir baking soda into buttermilk after butter is blended into dry ingredients. When buttermilk begins to foam, stir liquid into the dry ingredients to make a soft dough.

Fold in the currants on a lightly floured work surface, working the dough as little as possible. Proceed to roll out, cut, glaze, and bake the scones as indicated in the recipe above.

Drop Scones

The first scones were probably made as these are, dropped onto a hot griddle and baked quickly. They taste best split and eaten quite warm with butter and an intense flavor such as Apricot Orange Jam or Rhubarb Blackberry Jam (see Index).

YIELD: 12 SCONES

2 large eggs

5 tablespoons sugar

$^1/_2$ cup light cream

$1^1/_2$ cups cake flour

1 teaspoon baking powder

Preheat a griddle or heavy 12-inch skillet.

Beat the eggs and sugar together. Stir in the cream. Sift in the flour ½ cup at a time, adding the baking powder to the last addition, mixing each in thoroughly. (The scones will be the consistency of a thick pancake batter.)

Drop scones onto a hot griddle with a serving spoon (holds 2 tablespoons), and brown them on both sides for 5 to 6 minutes of total cooking time.

Serve hot immediately with marmalade and Crème Fraîche (see Index).

Giant Sunday Popover

This giant popover is easy to assemble so you'll have time to pour the juice, fry some bacon, and start the Sunday paper while you wait. Its transformation from batter to a puffed and rippled, crispy brown pastry, trailing the scent of vanilla, will awaken an appetite in even the groggiest diner.

YIELD: 6 SERVINGS

2 tablespoons salad oil

4 tablespoons unsalted butter

3 large eggs

$^3/_4$ cup milk

$^1/_4$ teaspoon vanilla extract

$^1/_4$ teaspoon salt

$^1/_2$ tablespoon sugar

$^3/_4$ cup unbleached flour, sifted before measuring

$^1/_4$ teaspoon ground cinnamon

$^1/_8$ teaspoon ground ginger

$^1/_4$ cup Vanilla Sugar (see p. 209)

1 cup Master Recipe for Fruit Sauce (see p. 245) made with Cranberry Orange Marmalade or Apple Red Raspberry Preserves

Preheat oven to 425° F. Combine oil and butter in an ovenproof 12-inch skillet. Put the skillet in the hot oven until butter begins to brown, 3 to 4 minutes.

Lightly beat the eggs with a whisk in a 2-quart bowl. Pour in the milk, vanilla, salt, and sugar, continuing to whisk gently. Sift the flour into a small bowl. Measure it, $^1/_4$ cup at a time, back into the sifter and onto the eggs and milk, whisking until each addition is just blended, though there may be small bits of unincorporated flour. Add the cinnamon and ginger to the last $1/4$ cup of flour.

Pour the batter into the hot skillet and return to oven to bake for 25 minutes. The popover will be puffed and brown. Dust the top with Vanilla Sugar and serve immediately in generous wedges. Pass warm Fruit Sauce at the table.

Apple Walnut Pancakes

YIELD: 6 SERVINGS

2 cups all-purpose flour

$^{1}/_{4}$ cup brown sugar

1 tablespoon baking powder

1 teaspoon salt

1 teaspoon cinnamon

$^{1}/_{2}$ teaspoon ground ginger

$^{1}/_{4}$ teaspoon grated nutmeg

1$^{1}/_{3}$ cups milk

1$^{1}/_{3}$ cups apple puree (*see* **Apple Pectin Stock, p. 103**)

2 large eggs

2 tablespoons walnut, *or* vegetable, oil

$^{2}/_{3}$ cup walnuts, toasted and coarsely chopped

Combine the dry ingredients: flour, brown sugar, baking powder, and seasonings in a mixing bowl and whisk together well. Make a well in the center. Combine the wet ingredients: milk, apple puree, eggs, and oil in a 1-quart measure and stir until well mixed. Pour the wet ingredients into the center of the dry mixture and blend until just mixed. Fold in the nuts.

Heat and lightly butter a large skillet. Ladle pancakes, using $^{1}/_{3}$ of the batter, onto the skillet, leaving room for the pancakes to spread. Turn when bubbles appear in the cakes or after 2 minutes. Cook another 2 minutes. Serve immediately or hold in a preheated 300°-F. oven while making the remaining pancakes.

Serve with tart or intensely sweet and bitter preserves: Red Raspberry Preserves or Orange Marmalade (see Index).

Apple Almond Waffles

YIELD: 6 WAFFLES

2 cups all-purpose flour

$^1/_4$ cup sugar

2 teaspoons baking powder

1 teaspoon baking soda

1 teaspoon sea salt

1 teaspoon allspice

1 cup buttermilk

$1^1/_2$ cups apple puree (*see* **Apple Pectin Stock, p. 103**)

2 large eggs

3 tablespoons butter, melted

$^2/_3$ cup toasted almonds, coarsely chopped

Preheat the waffle iron. Heat oven to 300° F.

Combine the flour, sugar, baking powder, baking soda, salt, and allspice in a mixing bowl and whisk together well. Make a well in the center. Combine the wet ingredients: buttermilk, apple puree, eggs, and butter in a 1-quart measure and blend together well. Pour the wet ingredients into the center of the dry mixture and stir until just mixed. Fold in the nuts.

Lightly oil the hot waffle iron. Ladle a scant cup of batter over the surface of the iron and gently close it. When the light on the iron goes off, indicating the waffle is cooked, carefully lift the waffle onto a bake sheet and place it in the preheated oven to stay warm while continuing to make the remaining waffles or serve immediately.

Russian Buckwheat Blinis with Blackberry Sauce

This is a fitting breakfast for those who rise early to spend a day roving in the country or working in the yard. The ingredients have a wild, wayside appeal. The buckwheat blinis are griddlecakes with a yeasty and slightly bitter taste. The blackberries retain their woodsy floral scent and some acidity even when sweetened. Together they refresh and invigorate an awakening palate.

YIELD: 12 BLINIS (4 SERVINGS)

Blinis

1 package active dry yeast *or* 2 $^{1}/_{2}$ teaspoons instant yeast

$^{1}/_{2}$ cup lukewarm water

$^{1}/_{2}$ cup each: unbleached white flour and buckwheat flour

$^{1}/_{2}$ teaspoon salt

$^{1}/_{2}$ cup milk

2 large eggs, separated

1 stick (4 ounces) unsalted butter, melted

Blackberry Sauce

$^{1}/_{3}$ cup sugar

1 cup water

1 cup Rhubarb Blackberry *or* Strawberry Blackberry Jam (pp. 39, 72)

Freshly squeezed lemon juice

Garnish

$^{1}/_{2}$ cup sour cream

BLINIS:

Dissolve the yeast in the water. Combine flours with salt in a 2-quart mixing bowl and make a well in the center. Pour in milk, egg yolks, and yeast mixture. Stir wet into dry ingredients to make a smooth batter.

Cover the bowl with plastic wrap and let rise for 2 hours at room temperature or refrigerate overnight. If refrigerated, allow the risen batter to warm for an hour at room temperature. Also warm egg whites to room temperature.

Heat a 12-inch skillet or griddle and coat it lightly with butter. Beat egg whites to soft peaks. Spoon 2 tablespoons melted butter and $\frac{1}{3}$ of egg whites onto the buckwheat batter and stir in gently. Fold in the remaining whites and butter in 2 parts.

Drop $\frac{1}{3}$ cup batter at a time onto the hot skillet and cook until the underside is browned, 2 to 3 minutes. Turn the blinis and cook another minute or two. Slip browned blinis onto a warm plate and hold them in the oven at 200° F. while preparing the rest.

BLACKBERRY SAUCE:

Make a simple syrup by combining the sugar and water in a saucepan and heating to a simmer. Cook the syrup for 5 minutes before stirring in the jam. Return mixture to a simmer. Season to taste with lemon juice.

GARNISH:

Serve blinis on warmed plates with Blackberry Sauce and a dab of sour cream.

French Toast with Plum Sauce

Day-old French bread is never wasted at our house. I turn it into an opportunity to enjoy French Toast, hot, puffed, and browned from the oven. We sprinkle each serving with Vanilla Sugar and pour on a sauce made from a fruit preserve with an assertive flavor and distinct fruit pieces, such as Plum Jam with Cardamom, Spicy Cranberry Jam, or Pear and Grape Preserves (see Index).

YIELD: 4–6 SERVINGS

French Toast

- 4 large eggs
- 1 tablespoon sugar
- $^1/_2$ teaspoon salt
- $^1/_4$ teaspoon each: ground cinnamon, nutmeg, ginger
- $^1/_4$ teaspoon vanilla extract
- 1 cup light cream
- 8–12 slices dry French bread (4–6 ounces)
- 3 tablespoons unsalted butter
- 2 tablespoons vegetable oil

Vanilla Sugar

- 1 6-inch-long vanilla bean
- 1 cup granulated sugar

Plum Sauce

- $^1/_3$ cup sugar
- 1 cup water
- 1 cup Plum Jam with Cardamom, Italian Plum Preserves, or Damson Plum Jam (see pp. 57, 168, 55)
- Freshly squeezed lemon juice

Preheat oven to 425° F.

FRENCH TOAST:

Lightly beat eggs with a fork in a jelly roll pan. Stir in sugar, salt, spices, and vanilla. Slowly pour in the cream, stirring to mix well.

Add the bread slices to this custard mixture and let them soak for 3 minutes on each side or until slices are saturated but still hold their shape.

Combine butter and oil in a 12-inch ovenproof skillet or pan. Place it in the hot oven to heat the fats. Lay the soaked slices in the hot fats, return skillet to the oven, and bake for 7 minutes. Turn slices over and bake another 7 minutes.

VANILLA SUGAR:

Snip the vanilla bean into $1/4$-inch segments over the sugar. Pulverize this mixture in a food processor or blender. Sift out the pieces of vanilla bean. Stored in an airtight container, vanilla sugar will keep, becoming more fragrant, for several months.

PLUM SAUCE:

Make a simple syrup by combining the sugar and water in a saucepan and heating to a simmer. Cook the syrup for 5 minutes before stirring in the jam. Return mixture to a simmer, and season to taste with lemon juice.

Serve French Toast hot from the oven, lightly sprinkled with Vanilla Sugar. Pass the Plum Sauce at the table.

Risen Biscuits

The combination of yeast and baking powder gives these biscuits a high rise and a light texture. The biscuit is firm in the hand and crumbles easily in the mouth. A berry preserve adds just the right amount of texture in the mouth and a wild, woodsy scent to this eating experience. My favorites include Four-Berry Preserves, Rhubarb Blackberry Jam, and Blueberry Raspberry Preserves (see Index).

If you make the variation of this recipe with fresh herbs, serve the biscuits with a wine or herb jelly (see pages 14, 15).

YIELD: 14 BISCUITS

1 package active dry yeast *or* 2 $^1/_2$ teaspoons instant yeast

$^1/_4$ cup warm water (100° F.)

$^1/_2$ tablespoon sugar

2 $^1/_2$ cups all-purpose flour

$^1/_2$ teaspoon salt

$^1/_2$ teaspoon baking powder

$^1/_2$ teaspoon baking soda

$^1/_3$ cup shortening

$^3/_4$ cup buttermilk at room temperature

1 stick unsalted butter (4 ounces), melted

Dissolve the yeast in water with the sugar. Combine flour, salt, baking powder, and baking soda in a 4-quart mixing bowl. Cut in the shortening to make a fine, mealy texture with the dry ingredients. Pour on the foamy yeast and buttermilk and beat into a stiff dough. Turn the ball of dough out onto a lightly floured work surface and knead by hand 1 to 2 minutes, until it is taut and springy. Cover and let dough rest for 15 minutes. (If using a food processor, cut shortening into dry ingredients with rapid on-and-off motions. Add yeast and buttermilk, then process until dough starts to ball. Knead by hand.)

210

Roll the dough out ½ inch thick, and cut it into 2-inch rounds with a biscuit cutter. Baste half the biscuit rounds with melted butter. Place the other biscuit rounds on top. Arrange biscuits 2 inches apart on a buttered and floured baking sheet. Cover them with plastic wrap and let rise in a warm, draft-free place for 1 hour.

Preheat oven to 375° F. Bake for 12 minutes or until richly browned and biscuits register 200 degrees internally on an instant-read thermometer. Cool the biscuits briefly on a wire rack and serve warm.

VARIATION

Risen Herb Twist Biscuits

YIELD: 14 BISCUITS

Biscuit Dough (see preceding recipe)
1 large egg yolk beaten with 1 tablespoon water
½ cup minced fresh herbs
½ teaspoon dried thyme, powdered
½ teaspoon powdered ginger

Prepare the biscuit dough, using preceding recipe excluding the butter. Roll the biscuit dough into an 8 x 12-inch rectangle. Brush the beaten egg yolk over the entire surface and sprinkle on the herbs and ginger. Roll up the dough along its wider side, brushing more yolk mixture on the exposed underside of the dough as it is rolled up.

Tightly pinch the edge closed. Slice the biscuit roll into 14 pieces with a sharp knife. Space the rolls 2 inches apart on a prepared baking sheet, cover with plastic wrap, and let them rise in a warm, draft-free place for 1 hour.

Brush the biscuits with the remaining egg yolk mixture and bake as directed in the Risen Biscuits recipe above.

English Muffins

Homemade English Muffins, eaten warm, are simply light years away from the dry sponges that pose as muffins in the supermarket. They are so simple to assemble, it's a wonder homemade muffins aren't the norm. Of all the breads tested for this book, this was my family's favorite.

It's their yeasty aroma and chewy texture that make English Muffins unique. I serve them with any of the preserves that have texture and tangy flavor.

YIELD: 12 ENGLISH MUFFINS

> 1 **package active dry yeast** *or* **2 ¹/₂ teaspoons instant yeast**
> 1 **tablespoon sugar**
> ³/₄ **cup warm water**
> 1 **cup milk**
> 3 **cups unbleached white flour**
> 2 **teaspoons salt**

Dissolve yeast and sugar in ¹/₂ cup warm water (100° F.) in the work bowl of a mixer or large mixing bowl. Warm the milk to tepid (70° F.). Add the milk, flour, and salt to the bowl. Beat at medium speed with a paddle attachment or by hand as a dough forms. Watch to see that the dough sticks equally to the beaters or hand-held spatula and the sides of the bowl. If the consistency is stiffer, add some of the remaining water. Beat for 3 minutes by hand or in an electric mixer until the dough is quite elastic.

Let the dough rise, covered, in a protected place at about 75° F. until it doubles in size. This will take about 1 hour.

Heat a cast-iron griddle or heavy aluminum 12-inch skillet. Oil the interior of several muffin rings and fit them into the skillet. (You can make your own rings from pet food tins by removing the tops and bottoms.)

Punch down the risen dough and tear off a $^1/_3$-cup piece. It will be sticky and stretchable. Place it in a muffin ring on the hot surface. Fill remaining rings the same way.

Bake muffins 10 minutes on each side and continue turning at 5-minute intervals until an instant-read thermometer inserted through the center of the muffin registers 200° F. Release the muffins from the rings, re-oil, and continue baking muffins. Let muffins cool for 15 minutes on a wire rack, pull them apart with fingers or fork, and serve warm with sweet butter and preserves.

ENGLISH MUFFIN VARIATIONS

Whole-Wheat English Muffins

Substitute 1 cup whole-wheat flour for 1 cup of the unbleached white flour in the master recipe above. Follow the same directions as for the master recipe.

Buckwheat English Muffins

Substitute $^1/_2$ cup each buckwheat and whole-wheat flour for 1 cup of the unbleached white flour in the master recipe above. Follow the same directions as for the master recipe.

English Muffins with Yogurt

One way to flatter a sweet preserve is to serve it with a slightly tart bread. Instead of making a sourdough bread, which is a considerable undertaking, I added feta cheese and yogurt to the easy English Muffin recipe. When you eat this yogurt muffin along with sweet butter, savor the added dimension its lightly sour element brings to this yeasty, chewy bread. Serve it with Strawberry Preserves or Italian Plum Preserves (see Index).

  1 tablespoon active dry yeast

  1 tablespoon sugar

  1 cup warm water, divided

1^1/$_2$ cups bread flour

1^1/$_2$ cups unbleached white flour

  2 teaspoons salt

  4 ounces feta cheese, grated

  1 cup plain yogurt

Dissolve yeast and sugar in ½ cup warm water (100° F.). Combine flours and salt in a 3-quart bowl. Make a well in the center of the dry ingredients and add grated cheese, yogurt, yeast mixture, and remaining water. Gradually stir dry ingredients into the wet to make a thick batter. When stirred, the dough will stick in equal parts to the stirring tool and the sides of the bowl. Beat by hand or in an electric mixer for 3 minutes, until the dough is quite elastic.

Let the batter rise, covered, in a protected place at about 75° F. until it doubles in size. This will take about 1 hour.

Follow cooking directions given in master recipe above.

9

DESSERTS

Homemade fruit preserves are just too tasty to be limited to the breakfast or tea table. They offer a head start, an inspiration really, for any number of dessert preparations. In this chapter, I start with the simplest use of preserves possible: sauces. After you thin a jam with Simple Syrup, it is ready-made as a topping for fruit, ice cream, or cake. I've provided some combinations to get you started.

A fruit preserve doesn't have to sit on a plate either. If you offer an English gentleman of a certain age a goblet filled with preserves loosely folded in whipped cream, he'll thank you for remembering his fondness for an old-fashioned Fruit Fool, one like his mother used to make. The French slather sweet crêpes with jam to eat on the street or flame with cognac for a dressy dessert presentation. On this side of the Atlantic, a rich Blueberry Sauce enlivens the classic American cheesecake.

It may come as a surprise to learn that fruit preserves can also be transformed into ingenious fountain treats. They offer an interesting texture and concentrated flavor when frozen. Take your pick of an addition of sugar syrup to make a sorbet or light cream or egg custard for ice cream. The master recipes in this chapter have freezing directions for those with and those without an ice cream machine.

I was inspired by traditional British sweets to include recipes for baked bread puddings and a showy fruit trifle in this collection. These desserts involve several simple recipes combined to make a showy presentation. Some are served warm, others cold—either way, they are timeless comfort foods. If lightness is your preference, try the Souffléed Pudding made with marmalade (page 226). I don't know which is more impressive, its magical rise in the oven or the length of time it stays puffed after you've removed it.

Legend has it that British housewives get competitive when it comes to preserving. They love to showcase their preserving prowess by filling a single pastry with as many as seven jams in a lattice crust. My own twenty-first-century Jam Tart (page 235) is quite modest by comparison. The Linzer Torte recipe (page 240), however, is unrepentantly "old school" and rich.

Fresh Pears with Blackberry Sauce

This is a wonderful last-minute dessert for family and guests. If you have time to prepare the pears an hour or two before dinner, the syrup will protect their color and freshness in the refrigerator. The sauce is so easy that it invites improvisation with an infusion of lemon verbena or mint.

YIELD: 6 SERVINGS

- 6 **firm, ripe Bartlett,** *or* **Bosc, pears**
- 2 **cups Simple Syrup (see p. 244)**
- ²/₃ **cup Blackberry Ginger Preserves, No-Sugar Apple Blackberry Jam,** *or* **Blueberry Blackberry Preserves (see pp. 171, 81, 159)**
- 2 **tablespoons blackberry brandy** *or* **1 teaspoon fresh lemon juice**

Peel and halve the pears. Remove stems and blossom ends with a paring knife. Scoop out cores with the small cup of a melon-baller. Lay pear halves in a shallow bowl filled with Simple Syrup. Coat them well and chill. (This may be done 2 to 3 hours in advance but not the night before.)

When ready to serve, combine, in a small skillet, the preserves with ⅓ cup of the syrup covering the pears. Warm and stir to make a smooth sauce. Add the brandy or lemon juice and simmer 30 seconds. Drain the pears and divide them among 6 dessert bowls. Spoon the warm fruit sauce over the pears and serve immediately.

Baked Peach Halves with Blueberry Sauce

When Michigan peaches appear at the farmers' markets in August, I always search out a few large, impeccably ripe beauties to bake. They seem to sweeten in the oven, with their stuffing of nuts, blueberries, macaroon crumbs, and a black currant liqueur from Dijon, France, called cassis. Served at room temperature with a warm, delicate blueberry sauce, these peaches are summer eating at its best.

YIELD: 6 SERVINGS

2 tablespoons chopped pecans

6 ripe Freestone peaches

$^{1}/_{3}$ cup crumbled macaroon cookies

$^{1}/_{4}$ cup fresh blueberries

3 tablespoons crème de cassis, divided

Sauce

$^{1}/_{2}$ cup Spicy Blueberry Preserves *or* Blueberry Jam with Mint (see pp. 161, 60)

2 tablespoons Simple Syrup (see p. 244)

1 tablespoon fresh lemon juice

1 tablespoon crème de cassis

Preheat oven to 350° F. Toast the pecans on a baking sheet in the oven for 10 minutes. Cool on the bake sheet, coarsely chop, and reserve. Generously butter a large, shallow baking dish.

Halve the peaches, remove the pits, and enlarge the hollows in each half by scooping out 1 teaspoon of flesh with a melon-baller or grapefruit spoon. Crush together these small peach pieces with the macaroons,

220

add the warm pecans, blueberries, and 2 tablespoons of cassis. Fill the craters of each peach half with this stuffing.

Arrange peaches in the buttered baking dish so they are not touching. Baste each lightly, using a total of 1 tablespoon of cassis, and bake for 30 minutes. Remove peaches from the oven and let them cool in the pan.

SAUCE:

Warm the jam or preserves with the syrup in a small saucepan. Add the lemon juice and cassis. Serve the peaches at room temperature with the warm sauce.

Fresh Peach Melba

This is the perfect dessert to eat when the weather is hot and you have an excess of super-ripe peaches. The combination of flavors and temperatures is incomparable: cold, rich ice cream; sweet, fresh peaches; and warm, tart raspberries. It's a dessert I long for during the winter months.

YIELD: 6 SERVINGS

- 1 cup Red Raspberry Preserves (see p. 151 or 173)
- 1/3 cup Simple Syrup (see p. 244)
- 1–2 tablespoons raspberry brandy (optional)
- 6 ripe, Freestone peaches
- 1 pint vanilla ice cream

Heat preserves and syrup to a simmer in a skillet, stirring until smooth. Add brandy if desired. Allow the sauce to cool slightly.

Dip the peaches in boiling water for 30 seconds. Cool under running water, peel, halve to remove the stones, and thinly slice. Divide peach slices among 6 glass serving bowls or goblets. Place a generous scoop of ice cream on the fruit. Top each serving with 3 tablespoons warm raspberry sauce. Serve immediately.

Master Recipe for Fruit Sorbets

A homemade jam, diluted with Simple Syrup and frozen, becomes a silken sorbet worthy of a special occasion or summer party. There's no need for an ice cream freezer, either. This thinned preserve can be poured onto a baking sheet, left in the freezer compartment, and just two hours later scooped out soft-frozen into serving goblets. The concentrated nature of the preserves guarantees a supple, stick-to-the-tongue succulence. These sorbets also retain their shape well and do not separate in storage.

YIELD: 1 QUART

2 cups fruit jam, no-sugar jam, *or* berry preserve

2 cups Simple Syrup (see p. 244)

1 tablespoon (or more) fresh lemon, *or* lime, juice

Combine a jam or preserve with an equal volume of syrup. Stir them together. Add lemon or lime juice to balance the sweetness with a bit of tartness.

FREEZING WITHOUT AN ICE CREAM FREEZER

Freeze sorbet on a shallow baking sheet at 0° F. It will be soft-frozen within 2 hours. Spoon into goblets or sherbet glasses and serve immediately.

FREEZING WITH AN ICE CREAM FREEZER

Chill the sorbet. Stir it well and pour into an ice cream machine. Freeze it, following the instructions that come with the machine.

Master Recipe for Philadelphia-Style Ice Cream

This simple combination yields a light, fruit–forward ice cream. Preserves with a loose texture and assertive fruit flavor such as Nectarine Jam with Grand Marnier, Seedless Black Raspberry Jam, or Strawberry Blackberry Preserves (see pages 45, 37, 164) are ideal choices for this ice cream. If you don't consume it all the first day, keep it in the freezer until the next time you serve it, and it's creamy texture will return as it softens.

YIELD: 1 QUART

2 cups half-and-half (light cream)

1¹/₂ cups fruit jam *or* preserves

Stir half-and-half into jam or preserves.

FREEZING WITHOUT AN ICE CREAM FREEZER

Still-freeze on a shallow pan, tightly covered. Break up the semi-frozen cream with a fork after the first hour, and twice more at ¹/₂-hour intervals.

FREEZING WITH AN ICE CREAM FREEZER

Chill this mixture for 1 hour. Stir and freeze according to the instructions that accompany your ice cream freezer. Allow the soft-frozen ice cream to ripen in the freezer for 2 to 4 hours before serving.

Master Recipe for Preserves in Ice Cream Custard

Pair this recipe's creamy, yolk-enriched custard base with one of the more intense and luxurious fruit flavors, such as Four Berry Preserves, Peach Preserves with Raspberries, or Blueberry Jam with Mint (see Index).

YIELD: 3 ½ CUPS

1 cup half-and-half (light cream)
1 cup whipping cream
3 large egg yolks
1⅓ cups jam *or* preserves

Combine 1 cup half-and-half with 1 cup whipping cream in a heavy, non-reactive pan and heat to scalding (180° F.).

Beat the yolks lightly in a small bowl. Gradually pour in 1 cup hot cream mixture, stirring constantly. Return the yolk-enriched cream to the pan and cook briefly over low heat until the custard coats the spoon (170° F.). Sieve the custard into a bowl. Stir preserves into the hot liquid, and mix until it reaches a smooth consistency.

Refrigerate this base until it is thoroughly chilled, 2 to 4 hours. Freeze according to instructions below.

FREEZING WITHOUT AN ICE CREAM FREEZER
Still-freeze on a shallow pan, tightly covered. Break up the semi-frozen cream with a fork after the first hour, and twice more at ½-hour intervals.

FREEZING WITH AN ICE CREAM FREEZER
Stir and freeze according to the instructions that accompany your ice cream freezer. Allow the soft-frozen ice cream to ripen in the freezer for 2 to 4 hours before serving.

Lemon Amaretto Souffléed Pudding with Raspberry Sauce

The ethereal appearance and texture of this soufflé are deceptive. Without an extra egg white, common to soufflés, this pudding is quite sturdy. It emerges from its hot water bath fully puffed, with the staying power and rich flavor of a pudding.

YIELD: 4 SERVINGS

Soufflé

  $^2/_3$ **cup Lemon Ginger Marmalade (see p. 131)**

  $^2/_3$ **cup Simple Syrup (see p. 244)**

  3 **tablespoons Amaretto**

  2 **tablespoons cornstarch**

  4 **large eggs, separated, room temperature**

  3 **tablespoons sugar**

Raspberry Sauce

  I **10-ounce package frozen red raspberries in sugar syrup**

  $I^1/_2$ **tablespoons crème de cassis liqueur *or* superfine sugar**

  I **teaspoon strained fresh lemon juice**

  I2 **perfect red raspberries**

SOUFFLÉ:

Generously butter and sugar a 6-cup soufflé mold. Refrigerate it. Preheat the oven to 325° F.

Mix the Lemon Ginger Marmalade and syrup in a small saucepan. Dissolve the cornstarch in the Amaretto and stir into the pan. Heat this base, stirring constantly, until it reaches a simmer and thickens noticeably.

Turn the hot marmalade mixture into a 2-quart bowl. Stir in the egg yolks, one at a time.

Beat egg whites with 2 tablespoons sugar to soft peaks. Add remaining sugar to make a firm meringue. Stir 1/3 of the whites into the marmalade mixture. Fold in remaining whites in two parts.

To fold, use a circular motion with a rubber spatula straight down into the center of the whites, flat along the bottom, and up the side, lifting whites to cover the ingredients on the surface before returning to the center again. Turn this circle into a doughnut shape by turning the bowl and repeating this action until only streaks of the ingredient being added still show.

Gently spoon the mixture into the chilled mold. Place mold in a pan of boiling water to half the height of the mold and bake for 40 minutes. (Soufflé may be held in the refrigerator for 30 minutes before baking.)

SAUCE:

Defrost the raspberries and sieve the berries with their syrup to remove the seeds. Stir in the cassis, or superfine sugar, and lemon juice. Refrigerate until serving time.

Serve soufflé hot at the table. Surround each serving with cool raspberry sauce and a few fresh berries.

Orange Marmalade Souffléed Pudding with Grand Marnier Sauce

YIELD: 4 SERVINGS

For the Soufflé, substitute ⅔ cup Orange Marmalade II (see page 124) for Lemon Ginger Mamalade. Stir the cornstarch into Grand Marnier instead of Amaretto, and proceed as described above.

For the Sauce, stir 2 tablespoons Grand Marnier into ¼ cup Crème Fraîche (page 250), and spoon a dollop onto each serving.

Master Recipe for Crêpes

YIELD:12–14 CRÊPES (6–7 SERVINGS)

    2 large eggs

    1 cup milk

$^1/_3$ cup water

    1 cup all-purpose flour

    2 tablespoons sugar

    1 teaspoon vanilla extract

$^1/_4$ teaspoon sea salt

    3 tablespoons melted butter, divided

In the work bowl of a processor or blender, combine the eggs, milk, water, flour, sugar, vanilla, salt, and 2 tablespoons melted butter. Run the machine for 5 seconds or until mixture is smooth. Scrape down the sides of the bowl and process briefly again. Pour into a large measure, cover, and refrigerate at least 1 hour or up to 24 hours. Before using, stir briefly to blend ingredients.

Heat a 6-inch non-stick crêpe pan or shallow skillet. Brush on a bit of the remaining tablespoon of butter. Pour in 3 tablespoons of batter (a scant $^1/_4$ cup) and immediately tilt the pan to allow the batter to coat the bottom. Cook the crêpe for 2 minutes until it becomes opaque and small bubbles form underneath it. Loosen the dried and crisp edges, invert the skillet over a plate, and allow the crêpe to drop onto it. Smooth it out and let it cool. Repeat with remaining batter, brushing on more butter as needed and stacking the completed crêpes on the plate.

Crepes may be held at room temperature, plastic wrapped, for 2 to 3 hours or refrigerated for 2 days.

Berry Jam Crêpes Flambées

YIELD: 12 CRÊPES (6 SERVINGS)

Crêpes

    1 **Master Recipe for Crêpes (p. 229)**

    ³/₄ **cup berry jam, any kind**

Syrup and Assembly

    1 **cup water**

    ¹/₂ **cup sugar**

    4 **tablespoons cognac** *or* **berry-flavored liqueur**

    1 **cup mixed berries**

Garnish

    1 **cup lightly whipped cream**

CRÊPES:

Prepare crêpes as instructed in Master Recipe (page 229). Spread 1 tablespoon of berry jam (any kind) over half of each crêpe. Fold the other half over, then fold the crêpe in half again to create a pie-shaped wedge. Repeat with remaining crêpes.

SYRUP AND ASSEMBLY:

Combine water and sugar in a large skillet and bring to a simmer, stirring to dissolve the sugar. Cook for 1 minute.

Place the crêpe wedges in the warm syrup over low heat. Turn them in the syrup to coat. Pour on the cognac (or berry-flavored liqueur) and ignite immediately. When flames have died down, divide the crêpes among 6 plates. Add the berries to the skillet and shake the pan to coat them with syrup.

GARNISH:

Spoon berries, with syrup, onto each serving and add a dollop of whipped cream.

Bread and Jam Pudding

This version of the classic bread pudding is a reminder that we never outgrow the need to be comforted by the pleasures of childhood. Pudding with bread, jam, and custard brings back the simple flavors of an indulged palate.

YIELD: 8–10 SERVINGS

2 large eggs

2 large egg yolks

$^1/_4$ teaspoon salt

$^1/_2$ teaspoon vanilla extract

1 tablespoon sugar

$1^1/_2$ cups half-and-half (light cream)

$1^1/_2$ cups milk

18–24 slices day-old French bread (10–12 ounces)

$1^1/_4$ cups jam such as Rhubarb Blackberry, Cherry Red Raspberry, Seedless Black Raspberry, *or* Strawberry Rhubarb (see pp. 39, 33, 37, 26)

Garnish with Crème Fraîche (see p. 250) and fresh berries *or* fruit slices to match the preserves (optional)

Generously butter an 8 x 12-inch gratin dish. Preheat the oven to 350° F.

Assemble the custard in a 2-quart bowl, adding the ingredients, from eggs to milk, in the order they are listed. Whisk the eggs and yolks together well, stir after seasonings have been added, and stir again as cream and milk are poured.

Place half the bread slices at the bottom of the gratin dish. Trim pieces to fill in spaces between slices, as needed. Cover the slices with half the custard. When the custard has soaked in, generously spread the bread with jam. Repeat with the second layer.

Allow the bread to sit for 10 minutes to completely absorb the custard. Cover the dish with foil buttered on the side facing the pudding. Bake for 30 minutes. Remove and turn the oven heat up to 375° F. Remove the foil and bake another 10 minutes.

Let the pudding cool to warm before serving. Accompany with Crème Fraîche and fresh fruit or berry pieces, if desired.

Orange Bread Pudding

The idea of a dessert combining sweet, sour, and bitter flavors in a creamy pudding was inspired by a most satisfying cabinet pudding I was served at the Jovan restaurant in Chicago 30 years ago. A dark stratum of rye bread woven into the white added sour overtones to the creamy, custard-saturated loaf. The pudding floated in a lightly bitter caramel and sherry sauce studded with raisins.

YIELD: 10 SERVINQS

1 recipe English Custard (see p. 249) made with $^1/_4$ cup Grand Marnier

12 ounces day-old white sandwich bread, crusts trimmed

8 ounces day-old seedless rye bread, crusts trimmed, cut into $^1/_2$-inch cubes

1 cup Orange Marmalade (see pp. 123, 124)

$^1/_2$ cup sherry, divided

1 cup whipped cream *or* Crème Fraîche (see p. 250)

Generously butter an 8 x 12-inch gratin dish. Preheat the oven to 350° F.

Make the custard, adding the Grand Marnier in place of the vanilla.

Generously spread the white bread slices with marmalade. Line the bottom and one-third up the sides of a 2$^1/_2$-quart decorative glass baking dish with about $^1/_2$ of the bread slices, marmalade sides facing up.

Add half the rye cubes and sprinkle with $^1/_4$ cup sherry. Pour on $^3/_4$ cup English Custard. Lay the remaining sandwich bread slices over this. Add the remaining rye cubes, $^1/_4$ cup sherry, and 1 cup custard. Lay on a final covering of white bread slices, marmalade sides down, and pour on the remaining custard.

Allow the dish to sit for 20 minutes so the bread can absorb the custard. Bake, covered with buttered foil, for 30 minutes in the upper half of the oven. Remove from the oven and uncover. Return to the oven and turn up the heat to 375. Bake another 10 minutes. Let the pudding cool to warm before serving. Serve with whipped cream or Crème Fraîche and fresh fruit or berry pieces, if desired.

Jam Tart

A tart filled with one of your own preserves and garnished with fresh fruit offers an unusually tasty and light pastry. If the preserver's well-stocked larder includes a homemade jelly with which to glaze the fresh tart, the effect is professional. A sprinkling of confectioners' sugar will work as a finishing touch as well.

YIELD: 8–12 SERVINGS

1 pre-baked 11-inch Tart Shell Pastry (see p. 246)

1$^1/_2$ cups (12 ounces) jam, preserves, or marmalade (see list below)

Whole fruit, thinly sliced, *or* 1 pint berries (see list below)

$^1/_3$ cup melted Red Currant *or* Cinnamon Cranberry Apple Jelly (see pp. 101, 99) for glaze *or* confectioners' sugar

Preheat the broiler if using a jelly glaze.

Spread the preserves in an even layer on the pre-baked tart shell in a springform pan. Prepare fruit complementary to the filling: peel, core, and thinly slice apples; peel and cut segments from oranges or grapefruits; cut other fruits or berries into bite-sized pieces. Spread slices in a layered wreath over the preserves. Dot whole berries over the top.

Brush the fruits lightly with melted jelly. Turn the removable outer rim of a springform pan on top of the tart so a ring of metal covers the edges of the crust or they will burn in the broiler. Slide the tart under the broiler until it browns lightly. Remove the springform protector, and cool the tart to room temperature before serving.

If using confectioners' sugar, eliminate the oven broiling. Simply shake on the sugar and serve.

SUGGESTED FLAVOR COMBINATIONS (see Index for recipes)

1. Apple Red Raspberry Preserves with thin apple slices and fresh raspberries. Glaze with Cinnamon Cranberry Apple Jelly.

2. Apple Grape Preserves with apple slices and Cinnamon Cranberry Apple Jelly glaze.

3. Any of the berry preserves or jams with fresh berries and Red Currant Jelly glaze.

4. Kiwifruit Mint Jam with kiwifruit and strawberry slices and Cinnamon Cranberry Apple Jelly.

5. Raspberry Pear Jam with pear slices and Cinnamon Cranberry Apple Jelly.

6. Orange Marmalade with orange segments and strained marmalade glaze instead of jelly.

7. Orange Cranberry Marmalade with orange segments and Cinnamon Cranberry Apple Jelly.

8. Grapefruit Marmalade with grapefruit segments and strained marmalade glaze instead of jelly.

Rhubarb Ginger Fool

The English gave the name fruit fool to a light bit of fruity dessert at the end of a meal. It's rich with heavy cream and tart with rhubarb, a replacement for the hard-to-find gooseberry used in the original. A fruit fool is an easy way to surprise your guests with a festive and refreshing finale to a spring or summer meal.

YIELD: 6 SERVINGS

- 1 cup Rhubarb Ginger Jam
- $^1\!/_3$ cup Simple Syrup (see p. 244)
- Fresh lemon juice
- $1^1\!/_2$ cups whipping cream (see note)
- 2 tablespoons crystallized ginger, cut into thin strips

Combine the jam, syrup, and just enough lemon juice to accent sweet and spicy flavors.

Beat the cream to soft peaks and spoon it into a 1-quart decorative glass bowl. Fold the jam mixture into the cream, leaving streaks of pink to alternate with white. (To fold, make a circular motion with a rubber spatula straight down into the center of the whipping cream, proceed flat along the bottom, and then go up the sides, lifting whites to cover the jam. Turn this circle into a doughnut shape by turning the bowl and repeating this action until the ingredients are mixed.)

This recipe can be made 2 to 3 hours ahead and held refrigerated in a serving bowl or in individual goblets. Scatter on ginger strips at serving time.

Note: Look for whipping, or heavy, cream that is pasteurized. Ultra-pasteurized whipping cream will not whip properly.

Blueberry Pecan Cheesecake

Homemade preserves and textured jams make delicious garnishes for cheesecake.
This recipe is my standby cake, and it can serve as a model for any number of your
own improvisations.

YIELD: 16–20 SERVINGS

Crust

- ¹/₂ cup pecan halves
- 10 ounces pecan sandie cookies
- 4 tablespoons unsalted butter, melted

Filling

- 1 cup sugar
- 1 teaspoon salt
- 3 tablespoons flour
- 2 pounds cream cheese *or* Neufchâtel
- 1¹/₂ teaspoons vanilla extract
- 3 large eggs
- 2 cups sour cream

Topping

- 1¹/₂ cups (12 ounces) Spicy Blueberry Preserves, Blueberry Jam with Mint, *or* Blueberry Blackberry Preserves (see pp. 161, 60, 159)

Preheat oven to 350° F. Toast the pecans for 10 minutes. Cool.

CRUST:

Reduce the cookies and pecans to fine crumbs in a food processor or blender with rapid on-and-off motions. Sprinkle on the butter and process for 5 seconds. Press crust mixture into the bottom and up two-thirds of the sides of a 9-inch springform pan. Refrigerate the pan while assembling the filling.

FILLING:

Measure sugar, salt, and flour into a 1-quart bowl. Stir ingredients together until they are well blended. Place cream cheese in a mixing bowl or work bowl of either an electric mixer or food processor. Process the cheese until smooth. Mix in the vanilla and the eggs, one at a time, stirring to keep mixture smoothly blended. Work in the sour cream one cup at a time.

Add dry ingredients to the filling and stir for 1 minute by hand, 30 seconds in a mixer, or 15 seconds in a food processor. Scrape down the sides of the bowl. Pour the filling into the chilled crust and bake for 50 minutes. The cake's top should be puffed, firm, and lightly browned.

Cool the cake on a wire rack for 30 minutes. Run a knife along the inside of the collar before releasing and removing it. When cake has come to room temperature, chill it until serving time.

TOPPING:

Spread preserves over the top of the cake. Chill for 30 minutes before serving.

CHEESECAKE VARIATIONS

Use the same cake filling as in the preceding recipe but substitute a different cookie for the crust (omit the pecan halves). Select a preserve topping that flatters this new cake and crust combination. Try the combinations below or invent your own.

1. Any of the ginger-spiced jams, such as Rhubarb Ginger Jam or Blackberry Ginger Preserve (see Index), would be terrific with a gingersnap cookie crust.

2. Tropical Pineapple Preserves (see Index), with its pure vanilla accent, would taste great in tandem with a rich vanilla wafers crust.

Linzer Torte

This famous Austrian pastry is a great way to showcase any of your homemade preserves, especially those with raspberries. To heighten the fresh raspberry flavor, I have substituted hazelnuts for almonds, usually added to the crust. These nuts, known as filberts in the U. S., have a sweetness that pairs beautifully with the tart raspberries.

YIELD: 10–12 SERVINGS

Pastry

  1 cup raw hazelnuts (5 ounces)
1$^1/_2$ cups unbleached flour
 $^1/_8$ teaspoon cloves
 $^1/_4$ teaspoon cinnamon
 $^1/_3$ cup sugar
     Grated zest of 1 lemon
  1 cup unsalted butter (2 sticks)
  2 ounces cream cheese
  2 large egg yolks
 $^1/_2$ tablespoon vanilla extract

Filling

1$^1/_2$ cups Red Raspberry Preserves, Four-Berry Preserves, *or* Cherry Red Raspberry Jam (see pp. 173, 169, 33)

Glaze

  1 large egg yolk
  2 teaspoons cream

Garnish

 $^1/_4$ cup confectioners' sugar

240

Butter the bottom and sides of a 9-inch springform pan. Preheat oven to 350° F. Toast the hazelnuts in the oven for 10 minutes. Rub the warm nuts in a tea towel to remove their brown skins.

PASTRY ASSEMBLY BY HAND:

Crush the nuts in a mortar and pestle. Blend with the dry ingredients. Allow the butter and cream cheese to come to room temperature. Cream them with egg yolks and vanilla, then work in the dry ingredient mixture.

PASTRY ASSEMBLY IN A FOOD PROCESSOR:

Pulverize the nuts with the other dry ingredients, using rapid on-and-off pulses in a processor. Quarter the sticks of butter lengthwise and cut each stick into 8 pieces across. Cut the cream cheese into teaspoon-sized bits. Blend these cold ingredients, along with the egg yolks and vanilla, into the dry ingredients until a dough begins to form.

Shape the dough into a flat disk, lightly flour it, wrap it airtight in plastic, and chill for 1 hour. Remove the dough from the refrigerator. Cut off ⅓ of the dough, wrap it, and return it to the refrigerator. Press the larger piece of dough evenly into the bottom and all the way up the sides of the springform pan with your fingers.

FILLING:

Spread the preserves on the dough. Remove the remaining piece of dough from the refrigerator, and roll it about ¼ inch thick on a lightly floured surface. Cut ½-inch strips and lay some parallel at 1½-inch intervals over the preserves. Turn the pan 90 degrees and repeat the parallel strips to form a lattice. Use a paring knife to bend the dough above the preserves layer and away from the sides of the pan. Press the strips onto the dough at the edge of the pan to make a thick border around the pan, sealing and framing the lattice.

GLAZE:

Beat together the egg yolk and cream. Baste all pastry surfaces with this glaze and refrigerate the torte for ½ hour.

Bake for 45 minutes or until the torte is richly browned. Let it cool 10 minutes before removing the springform sides. Slide the torte off the pan bottom onto a serving tray when it has come to room temperature.

GARNISH:

Dust the top with confectioners' sugar

Strawberry Trifle

Surprise your dinner guests by first announcing you have "just a trifle" for dessert. Then bring in this stunning creation of jam-spiraled sponge cake filled with a rich vanilla custard and topped with whipped cream. Don't you love the English knack for understatement?

YIELD: 10 SERVINGS

1 sheet Jelly Roll Sponge Cake (see p. 247)

$^1/_2$ cup medium-sweet sherry, divided

$1^1/_2$ cups Strawberry Preserves (see p. 163)

$1^1/_2$ recipes of English Custard (see p. 249)

1 cup whipped cream

Remove the waxed paper protecting the top surface of the cake. Trim crusty edges, and sprinkle the cake with 2 tablespoons of sherry.

Spread on the Strawberry Preserves, and use a long sheet of waxed paper under the cake to help roll up the cake along the long edge. Cut the jelly roll cake into 18 slices.

Tightly lay the jelly roll slices on the bottom and up the sides of a 2-quart glass serving bowl, reserving 6 slices for the top. Sprinkle the remaining sherry over the cake slices. Pour on the English Custard. Layer the top of the custard with the remaining jelly roll slices. Cover and chill at least 2 hours before serving. (It can be held for several hours or overnight.)

At serving time, with a rosette-tipped pipe, form a decorative pattern over the top of the trifle with whipped cream. You can also spoon out the trifle and add a dollop of whipped cream to each plate as it is served.

Simple Syrup

Simple Syrup is the cooked sugar and water medium that makes preserve-based sauces and frozen sorbets possible. The added tablespoon of lemon juice in the syrup plays a dual role as catalyst to dissolve the sugar and to balance the flavor.

3 cups water

1 cup granulated sugar

1 tablespoon strained fresh lemon juice

Combine water, sugar, and lemon juice in a heavy, non-reactive 2-quart saucepan. Heat, stirring occasionally, until the sugar dissolves. Let the syrup cool to room temperature and transfer it to a storage jar. It will keep, refrigerated, for as long as 2 months.

Master Recipe for Fruit Sauce Made from Jams and Preserves

Although proportions are specified in this recipe, you may use them with flexibility, thinning fruit preserves to the consistency you desire for each dessert. Add lemon juice one teaspoon at a time, tasting after each addition, until you reach a balance of sweet and sour elements.

YIELD: 2 CUPS

1 ¹/₂ **cups fruit jam or preserves**

¹/₂ **cup (or more) Simple Syrup (see p. 244)**

Fresh lemon juice to taste

Heat jam or preserves with ¹/₂ cup Simple Syrup in a heavy, non-reactive 1-quart saucepan, stirring constantly until the jam has thoroughly liquified into a sauce. Thin with additional syrup if the sauce is too thick to coat a spoon lightly and evenly. Off heat, add lemon juice by the teaspoon, tasting after each addition, to balance the sweetness of the sauce.

Serve warm or at room temperature with ice cream, fresh fruit, cakes, French toast, or blinis.

Tart Shell Pastry

YIELD: 1, 11-INCH SPRINGFORM TART SHELL

    1 vanilla bean (optional)
    3 ounces (6 tablespoons) unsalted butter at room
       temperature
  3/4 cup confectioners' sugar, sifted
    3 large egg yolks at room temperature
 1 3/4 cups unbleached flour, sifted, divided
  1/8 teaspoon sea salt
       Unsalted butter for buttering the pan

Slit open the vanilla bean lengthwise and scrape the seeds out into the
work bowl of a food processor or electric mixer. Add butter to the bowl
and process until smooth. Add the sugar and process until a thick creamy
paste forms. Add the egg yolks, process, scrape down the sides, and
process again until smooth. Add 1 1/2 cups flour and salt and process to
form a dough. If the mixture remains creamy, work in the remaining flour,
2 tablespoons at a time. The dough should break up into small balls.

Scrape the dough out of the bowl onto a lightly dusted sheet of waxed
paper. Lightly dust the top and flatten dough out into a disk. Wrap airtight
and refrigerate at least 1 hour, preferably overnight.

Thoroughly butter an 11-inch springform tart mold. Lightly flour the chilled
pastry and roll it out between sheets of waxed paper. Make the diameter
of the pastry 1 inch larger than the mold. Remove the top sheet of waxed
paper and invert the dough into the mold. Press the dough into the mold
carefully, pressing the edges of the dough against the side of the mold
without stretching it. Gently peel off the remaining sheet of waxed paper.
Trim the dough at the rim and prick it over the bottom. Chill the lined
mold at least 1 hour, or tightly wrap and chill overnight.

Preheat oven to 375° F. Remove any covering, place the mold on a baking
sheet, and bake for 20 to 30 minutes until the shell is lightly browned.
Cool on a rack.

Jelly Roll Sponge Cake

A light, lemon-scented sponge cake is the perfect partner for a filling of rich strawberry preserves. Once rolled, this cake can be layered in a trifle (see page 243), or serve it in a deconstructed fashion, with two overlapping slices on a dessert plate, surrounded by custard and a fresh berry garnish.

YIELD: 1 JELLY ROLL SPONGE CAKE

- **5 large egg whites at room temperature (scant ³/₄ cup)**
  Pinch of salt
- **1 cup granulated sugar, divided**
- **4 large egg yolks at room temperature**
- **³/₄ cup flour sifted before measuring**
- **1 teaspoon grated lemon rind**

Butter the bottom of a 10 x 15-inch sheet cake pan. Line it with waxed paper or parchment, and butter the paper. Preheat oven to 350° F.

Beat the egg whites at medium speed in a mixer to soft peaks, adding a pinch of salt and ¼ cup sugar at the start. Add the remaining sugar slowly, continuing to beat as the whites gain body and flexibility. Lightly beat the yolks with a fork and fold them into the whites by hand. To fold, make a circular motion with a rubber spatula straight down into the center of the whites, then flat along the bottom, and finally up the sides, lifting whites to cover the added ingredient on the surface before returning into the center again. Sift in the flour ¼ cup at a time, and gently fold it in, adding the grated lemon rind with the last of the flour.

Carefully spoon the batter onto the cake sheet. Level it with a flat spatula. Bake for 20 minutes or until the cake is puffed and golden. Let the cake cool in its pan on a rack. Loosen the cake around the edges and turn it onto a strip of lightly oiled waxed paper 6 inches longer than the length of the pan. (If you are not filling this cake immediately, roll it up and store it in an airtight plastic bag in the refrigerator or freezer.)

Strawberry Jelly Roll

Spread the cooled cake with Strawberry Preserves (page 163), and, using a long sheet of waxed paper under the cake, roll it up along the long edge. Wrap and refrigerate until serving time. Sprinkle with confectioners' sugar and cut into ¾-inch slices. Serve two overlapping slices on each plate with a fresh strawberry garnish. Surround the slices with spoonfuls of English Custard (recipe follows).

English Custard

This custard formula is rich in egg yolks for extra body and color. You may wish to substitute two tablespoons of a fruit brandy or liqueur per cup of custard in place of vanilla if you want the custard to complement a specific fruit flavor.

YIELD: 2 ½ CUPS

2 cups half-and-half cream

1 vanilla bean *or* **1 tablespoon pure vanilla extract**

6 egg yolks

½ cup sugar

¼ teaspoon salt

Pour the cream into a heavy, non-reactive 1 ½-quart saucepan. Cut through the outer peel of the vanilla bean along its length with a paring knife. Scrape out the contents and add the seeds and pod to the cream. (If using vanilla extract, see last paragraph.) Heat the cream to 180° F. This is the point when small bubbles appear at the edge of the pan and a skin forms over the cream.

While the cream is heating, whisk together egg yolks, sugar, and salt in a 2-quart bowl. Slowly pour 1 cup of the hot cream into the yolks, whisking vigorously. Return this mixture to the pan and heat, stirring constantly, until the custard coats the spoon, about 170° F.

Sieve the custard into a 1-quart measure and remove the vanilla bean pod. Dot the custard's surface with the end of a stick of unsalted butter to prevent a skin from forming. (After 15 minutes, stir in vanilla extract if you haven't used a vanilla bean and dot the surface again.) Cool custard to room temperature and refrigerate.

Crème Fraîche

This lightly cultured cream has a slightly tart flavor and the consistency of sour cream. The taste complements desserts made with fruit preserves, and its thick texture makes it an attractive garnish.

YIELD: 2 CUPS

2 cups whipping cream (not ultra-pasteurized)
2 tablespoons buttermilk

Heat the cream to 100° F. in a saucepan or microwave. Stir in the buttermilk. Pour mixture into a glass container with a lid that seals tightly. Keep the closed jar at room temperature, between 70° and 75° F., for 18 to 36 hours, until the cream has thickened noticeably. Refrigerate this cultured cream. It will continue to thicken, but more slowly in a colder temperature. Plan to use it within a month, and stir it well each time before pouring.

A SEASONAL GUIDE TO FRESH FRUITS AND VEGETABLES FOR PRESERVING

Each fruit is listed with the months it is in season. My resource was the "Supply Guide" from the United Fresh Fruit and Vegetable Association, which indicates the availability of produce at wholesale markets rather than their harvest times. Italicized months indicate seasonal peaks. Many of the ripeness profiles that follow the dating were supplemented by information from "The Greengrocer" by Joe Carcione. I describe the appearance of some fruits when they are under-ripe to encourage their use in small amounts (25%) to benefit acid and pectin content in jelly, marmalade, and preserves.

FRUITS

APPLES: All apples should be firm, well formed, glossy, and free of bruises and blemishes

    Cortland: September and October

    Golden Delicious: year 'round

    Granny Smith: all months except October

    Greening: October and November

    Jonathan: October to May

    Macintosh: October to June

APRICOTS: late May through *June, July,* and August

Firm, golden, fuzzy fruits are best. A touch of pink blush indicates they are approaching full ripeness.

BLACKBERRIES: June, *July, August,* and September

Look for plump, dark blackberries with long caps packed with juicy lobes.

BLUEBERRIES: June, *July,* and *August*

Berries that are full, round, and firm with a dusty bloom are best. Include a few with a reddish tinge, which indicates they are slightly underripe and good for preserving.

BOYSENBERRIES: June, *July,* and *August*

These look like giant blackberries. Both whole berries and clustered lobes are larger and fuller. They are also quite fragile. Avoid baskets stained with juice. Store berries in a single layer and use them within two days.

CHERRIES, SOUR: June and *July*

Cherries should be bright red, slightly soft to the touch, and unblemished, with green stems attached.

CRABAPPLES: July and *August*

These miniature round apples can vary in color from bright orange-gold to dark red. Select large, unflawed ones from the tree rather than the ground if you are harvesting them yourself.

CRANBERRIES: *October, November,* and December

Color is not as good an indicator of quality as the condition of the fruit. Berries should be oval, firm, and bright, free of dents and soft spots.

CURRANTS. RED: July

These small berries should be a rich translucent red, perfectly round and on the stem.

FIGS, DRIED: year 'round

Choose packages of golden Calimyrna or Calamata figs that are gently firm but not hard or dry to the touch.

GRAPEFRUIT, PINK AND WHITE: October through March
This fruit should be round, firm, and heavy for its size. Peel is best when bright yellow and fine grained.

GRAPES, CONCORD: September and October
Good bunches will have well-developed side branches packed with dark, plump grapes that carry a natural dusty bloom.

KIWIFRUIT: California: October through May
This brown fuzzy fruit is ready for the preserving pot when it is still quite firm, yielding only slightly to gentle finger pressure.

LEMONS: year 'round
Look for lemons that have a fine-grained skin and bright yellow color with a slightly greenish cast, which is a sign that they are barely ripe and wonderfully sour. Pick ones that are oval, firm, and feel heavy for their size.

LIMES: year 'round
They should have the same features as lemons: good shape (in this case, round), bright color, no blemishes, and fine grain. A slightly yellowish tinge to the skin indicates ripeness, so choose the less ripe green ones.

NECTARINES: June through September
Nectarines should be bright yellow-gold with a fine red blush, which indicates they are just ripe. They will also be slightly soft along the seam of the fruit. Pick ones that are plump, well-formed, and free of bruises.

ORANGES, NAVEL: most available November through May
Color is not as good a guide to fruit maturity as the feel of the orange in your hand. You want it to be firm, round, and heavy for its size. The skin should be fine grained and free from mold and blemishes.

PEACHES: May, June, *July, August,* and September

Make sure the peaches you buy have a uniform yellow cast, which indicates they were not picked green. They should be firm but yield a bit to gentle pressure and give off a rich peach fragrance.

PEARS, BARTLETT: August through October

Pears are picked green, and you can purchase them at an early stage of ripening to let them slowly turn golden in your kitchen at room temperature. Use them when they have just turned yellow and before their tender skins give slightly to gentle pressure.

PINEAPPLES: year 'round

The best signs of ripeness in a pineapple are a bright green crown and golden fruit color accompanied by a fragrant fruit scent. However, this ideally ripe pineapple is a rare find at the supermarket. You'll most likely have to sniff the scent at stem end because the fruit will still be cold from refrigeration. If you find one that is fresh-looking and smelling, with only the lower third golden and the rest green, take it. The pineapple will continue to ripen satisfactorily in your kitchen. Do not purchase any fruit with brown leaves, soft spots, or a spoiled smell. Also note that a large pineapple has a higher percentage of flesh than a small one.

PLUMS, DAMSON: August

Damsons are small, plump, and tender spheres of deep purple.

PLUMS, ITALIAN: July, August, and *September*

Ripe Italian plums have a slightly hazy bloom over their dusty purple skins, and their plump oval lobes give under the thin skin. Some can be used for preserving when they are still rather firm and reddish in hue.

QUINCES: September, October, and November

The quince is a hard, knobby fruit when ripe. Only a gold cast over a green peel and a luscious apple aroma give any indication of ripeness. Cook them before they begin to shrivel at the stem end and soften to the touch.

RASPBERRIES, RED AND BLACK: *July*, August, and September (black in July only)

The caps of ripe raspberries easily slip off the stem. The lobes are firm, plump, and a richly colored shade of red or glossy blue-black. Do not buy boxes stained with fruit. Slide them out of their boxes onto a flat tray in one layer and use within a day or two.

RHUBARB: year 'round but especially April and May

Although hothouse farming and summer gardens have made rhubarb available almost all year long, it still tastes best in the spring, when the first field crops are harvested. Deep red field rhubarb has a slightly tarter flavor than the lighter pink hothouse variety. Either is good for preserving as long as stalks are firm, moist, and free of cuts and bruises.

SERVICEBERRIES: June, *July*, and August

This is a crop you will have to pick yourself. The berries mature over the summer, becoming dark red and drier over time. They are best for preserving in late June and July. You may pluck them from the stem since they are small and not particularly juicy. Look for bright red color and round, plump shape.

STRAWBERRIES: April, May, and *June*

Strawberries do not have to be deeply red all over to be good for preserving. In fact, as many as 30 percent can be partly ripe. Small plump ones with bright green caps are preferred for preserves, though large berries may be halved or quartered, if necessary, for uniformity. You can store them as long as three days in a single layer in the refrigerator. Do not remove the caps or rinse them until you are ready to cook.

VEGETABLES

ONIONS: year 'round

Look for firm young onions. Those that ripen early in the season are usually sweeter than the latecomers. (You will have to ask your produce manager about the source and season of the onions when you buy them.) Onion skins should be dry, the flesh firm. Stay away from onions whose neck ends are soft, discolored, or sprouting green stems.

PEPPERS, BELL AND JALAPEÑO: year 'round

Bell and variety peppers can now be had many months of the year, though the jalapeño is more likely available at ethnic markets in the winter. Select peppers most brightly colored with a smooth, glossy surface. Turn them over in your hand to check for undesirable impact bruises and splits.

TOMATOES: ROUND VARIETIES: July, *August,* and *September*; ITALIAN PLUM: Late summer into fall

Tomatoes taste best when used fresh from the garden in late summer: red, ripe, and luscious. The best time to select green ones is at the end of the season, before they succumb to frost.

ZUCCHINI: year 'round

Like the other vegetables listed here, zucchini is now available most months of the year. Small zucchini are preferred because they are the tenderest throughout. Select ones with a deep green skin, symmetrical oblong shape, and firmness at both ends.

INDEX

A

Acid, role of in pectin jell, 6, 10
Apple
  Almond Waffles, 205
  Blackberry Jam, No-Sugar, 81
  Cinnamon Cranberry Apple
    Jelly, 99
  Cinnamon Muffins, 190
  Ginger Jam, 28
  Grape Jam, No-Sugar, 80
  Grape Preserves, 180
  Jam Tart, 235
  and Onion Marmalade, 136
  Pectin Stock, 9, 103
  Puree for Muffins, Waffles, and
    Pancakes, 104
  Raspberry Jam, No-Sugar, 91
  Red Raspberry Preserves, 176
  Strawberry Jam, No-Sugar, 88
  Walnut Pancakes, 204
Apricot
  Blueberry Jam, 40
  Citrus Marmalade with
    Apricots, 132
  Orange Jam, 41
  Pineapple Raspberry Jam with
    Apricots, No-Sugar, 83

B

baking techniques, 184, 185
Ball jars, 2
Banana Bran Muffins, 193
Berry Jam Crêpes Flambée, 230
Biscuits
  Herb Twist, Risen, 211
  Risen, 210

Blackberry
  Apple Blackberry Jam,
    No-Sugar, 81
  Blueberry Blackberry Preserves,
    159
  Ginger Preserves, 171
  Pears, Fresh, with Blackberry
    Sauce, 219
  Preserves with Lemon Zest,
    Quick, 152
  Rhubarb Blackberry Jam, 39
  Sauce, 207
  Strawberry Blackberry Jam, 72
  Strawberry Blackberry Preserves,
    164
Blinis, Russian Buckwheat with
  Blackberry Sauce, 206
Blueberry
  Apricot Blueberry Jam, 40
  Blackberry Preserves, 159
  Jam with Mint, 60
  Orange Jam, No-Sugar, 84
  Peach Blueberry Jam, 42
  Pear and Blueberry Jam,
    No-Sugar, 78
  Pecan Cheesecake, 238
  Pineapple Blueberry Jam, 46
  Preserves, Spicy, 161
  Raspberry Preserves, 175
  Rhubarb Jam, 62
  Sauce, 220
Boysenberry Jam, 61
Bread
  and Jam Pudding, 231
  Orange, Pudding, 233
  Zucchini, 195

Buckwheat
  Blinis, Russian, with Blackberry
    Sauce, 206
  English Muffins, 213
  Muffins, 191
Buttermilk Currant Scones, 200
Butter Pecan Muffins, 186

C

Cabernet Jelly, 105
Cake, Jelly Roll Sponge, 247
Cassis, Black Raspberry, Jam, 36
Chardonnay Jelly, 105
Cheesecake, Blueberry Pecan, 238
Cherry
  Cassis Preserves, Quick, 158
  Red and Black Raspberry Jam
    with Cherries, 35
  Red Raspberry Jam, 33
  Vanilla Jam, 34
Cinnamon
  Cranberry Apple Jelly, 99
  Lemon Lime Marmalade with
    Cinnamon, 129
  Nectarine Jam with Pineapple,
    No-Sugar, 82
  Strawberry Kiwifruit Jam, 70
Citrus
  and Green Pepper Marmalade,
    141
  Marmalade with Apricots, 132
  Marmalade, Quick-Mixed, 118
  Marmalade with Star Anise, 126
cold plate test for jell, 17
Cornmeal Muffins, 187
Crabapple Jelly, 98

Cranberry
Cinnamon, Apple Jelly, 99
Jam, Spicy, 54
Orange Cranberry Marmalade,
    Quick, 119
Cream Scones, 199
Crème Fraîche, 250
Crêpes
Berry Jam, Flambées, 230
Master Recipe for, 229
Currant, Black
Black Raspberry Cassis Jam, 36
Currant, Red
Jelly with Cardamom, 102
Jelly, Master Recipe for, 101
Jelly, Sweet and Hot, 102
Raspberry Red Currant
    Preserves, 174
Custard, English, 249

D
Damson Plum Jam, 55
doubling recipes, 20
Drop Scones, 200

E
English Custard, 249
English Muffins, 212
Buckwheat, 213
Whole-Wheat, 213
with Yogurt, 213
equipment, 6, 9–18

F
Fig
Orange Fig Jam, No-Sugar, 86
Rhubarb Fig Jam, 27
Four-Berry Preserves, 169
freezing ice cream, how to, 223
French Toast with Plum Sauce,
    208
frozen fruits, how to use, 19, 20
Fruit
preparing for preserves, 11, 12
Sauce Made from Jams and
    Preserves, Master Recipe for,
    245
Sorbets, Master Recipe for, 223
Fruit Fool, 217
funnels, use in preserving, 16

G
Giant Sunday Popover, 202
Ginger
Apple Ginger Jam, 28
Blackberry Ginger Preserves, 171
Lemon Ginger Marmalade, 131
Nectarine Plum Jam with
    Ginger, 71
Peach Jam, 66
Pear Jam, 29
Rhubarb Fool, 237
Rhubarb Ginger Jam, 38
Grape
Apple Grape Jam, No-Sugar,
    80
Apple Grape Preserves, 180
Jelly with Fresh Thyme, 97
Jelly, Master Recipe for, 96
Jelly, Spicy, 97
Pear and Grape Jam,
    No-Sugar, 85
Pear and Grape Preserves, 178
Pear and Grape Preserves,
    Quick, 157
Grapefruit
Citrus Marmalade with
    Apricots, 132
Citrus Marmalade with Star
    Anise, 126
Pink, Marmalade, Spicy, 121
Pink, Marmalade with Vanilla,
    Quick, 117
Quick-Mixed Citrus
    Marmalade, 118
Grape-Nuts® Muffins, 192
Green Tomato Jam, 53

H
herbs, use of in preserves, 14, 15
hot water bath, 18

I
ice cream, freezing of, 223
Ice Cream, Philadelphia-Style,
    Master Recipe for, 224
Italian Plum Preserves, 168

J
Jam Tart, 235

jams, 23–72
definition of, 5, 6
techniques for making, 23, 24
jams, no-sugar, 75–91
techniques for making, 75, 76
jar lifter, 18
jars
history of, 2, 3
how to fill, 15, 16
jell
how to stimulate, 19
point on thermometer, 13, 14
process, 5–10
testing for, 13, 14, 17
jellies, 93–111
definition of, 5
techniques for making, 93
Jelly Roll Sponge Cake, 247
Jelly Roll, Strawberry, 248

K
Kir Cocktail Jelly, 106
Kiwifruit
Mint Jam, 44
Pear Jam, No-Sugar, 89
Pineapple Jam, 43
Strawberry Kiwifruit Jam, 70
knives used in preserving, 11

L
Lemon
Amaretto Souffléed Pudding
    with Raspberry Sauce, 226
Blackberry Preserves with
    Lemon Zest, Quick, 152
Ginger Marmalade, 131
Lime Marmalade with
    Cinnamon, 129
in Orange Marmalades I and II,
    123, 124
Pineapple Lemon Preserves,
    Quick, 154
Zucchini Marmalade with Basil,
    139
lids, jar, in preserving, 15, 16
Lime
Lemon Lime Marmalade with
    Cinnamon, 129
Vanilla Marmalade, 128
Zucchini Marmalade, 138

Linzer Torte, 240
liqueurs, use of in preserves,
 14, 15

M

marmalades, 113–144 (*also see*
 Quick Marmalades)
 definition of, 5
 history of, 113
 techniques for making, 114, 115
Mason jars, 2
measuring utensils, 10
Mint
 Blueberry Jam with Mint, 60
 Jelly, 107
 Kiwifruit Mint Jam, 44
 Strawberry Kiwifruit Jam with
 Mint, 70
Mold, 16
Muffins (*also see* English Muffins)
 Apple Cinnamon, 190
 Banana Bran, 193
 Buckwheat, 191
 Butter Pecan, 186
 Cornmeal, 187
 Cornmeal, Country Style, 188
 English, 212, 213
 Grape-Nuts®, 192
 Marmalade, 194
 Oatmeal, 189

N

Nectarine
 Cinnamon Nectarine Jam with
 Pineapple, No-Sugar, 82
 Jam with Grand Marnier, 45
 Orange Jam, 64
 Plum Jam with Ginger, 71
no-sugar jams, 75–91
non-reactive pans, 12

O

Oatmeal Muffins, 189
Onion and Apple Marmalade, 136
Orange
 Apricot Orange Jam, 41
 Blueberry Orange Jam,
 No-Sugar, 84
 Bread Pudding, 233
 Cranberry Marmalade, Quick,
 119

Fig Jam, No-Sugar, 86
Marmalade I, 123
Marmalade, II, 124
Marmalade Souffléed Pudding
 with Grand Marnier Sauce,
 228
Marmalade, Thirty-Minute, 116
Nectarine Orange Jam, 64
Pineapple Jam, No-Sugar, 87
Tomato Orange Jam, 51
Zucchini Marmalade, 140

P

Pancakes, Apple Walnut, 204
pans used in preserving, 12
Pastry, Tart Shell, 246
Peach
 Blueberry Jam, 42
 Ginger Peach Jam, 66
 Halves, Baked, with Blueberry
 Sauce, 220
 Melba, Fresh, 222
 Pineapple Jam, 63
 Pineapple Jam with Apricots,
 No-Sugar, 77
 Preserves with Raspberries, 166
 Raspberry Jam, No-Sugar, 79
Pear
 and Blueberry Jam, No-Sugar,
 78
 Ginger Pear Jam, 29
 and Grape Jam, No-Sugar, 85
 and Grape Preserves, 178
 and Grape Preserves, Quick, 157
 Kiwifruit Pear Jam, No-Sugar,
 89
 and Pineapple Jam, 30
 and Plum Jam, 31
 Preserves with Pernod, Quick,
 156
 Raspberry Pear Jam, 32
Pears, Fresh, with Blackberry
 Sauce, 219
Pecan Blueberry Cheesecake, 238
Pectin, 3, 6–10, 19
 Apple Stock, 103
 "fix," when jelly won't jell, 19
 levels in fruits, 6–9
 levels, how to raise, 9, 10, 19
 Stock Using Greening Apples,
 104
 testing for, 8

Peppers
 Hot, Jelly, 109
 Ratatouille Marmalade, 143
 Red Bell, Marmalade, 134
 Sweet, Jelly, 108
Philadelphia-Style Ice Cream,
 224
Pineapple
 Blueberry Jam, 46
 Kiwifruit Pineapple Jam, 43
 Lemon Preserves, Quick, 154
 Orange Pineapple Jam,
 No-Sugar, 87
 Peach Pineapple Jam, 63
 Peach Pineapple Jam with
 Apricots, No-Sugar, 77
 Pear and Pineapple Jam, 30
 Preserves, Quick Tropical, 153
 Raspberry Jam with Apricots,
 No-Sugar, 83
 Strawberry Pineapple Jam,
 No-Sugar, 90
Plum
 Damson Plum Jam, 55
 Italian Plum Preserves, 168
 Jam with Cardamom, 57
 Nectarine Plum Jam with
 Ginger, 71
 Pear and Plum Jam, 31
 Sauce, 208
Popover, Giant Sunday, 202
preserves, 147–181 (*also see* Quick
 Preserves)
 cooking, 12–15
 definition of, 5
 history of, 1–3, 147, 183
 in Ice Cream Custard, Master
 Recipe for, 225
 many uses of, 217, 218
 techniques for making, 147–149
preserving jars and lids, 2, 3, 10,
 11, 15, 16
Prune Tomato Jam, 47
Pudding
 Bread and Jam, 231
 Lemon Amaretto Souffléed,
 with Raspberry Sauce, 226
 Orange Bread, 233
 Orange Marmalade Souffléed,
 with Grand Marnier Sauce,
 228

Q

Quick Marmalades, 116–120
Quick Preserves, 150–158
Quince Jam, 58

R

Raspberry, Black
Raspberry Cassis Jam, 36
Raspberry Jelly, 100
Red and Black Raspberry Jam
with Cherries, 35
Seedless Black Raspberry Jam,
37
Serviceberry and Wild Black
Raspberry Jam, 68
Raspberry, Red
Apple Raspberry Jam,
No-Sugar, 91
Apple Red Raspberry Preserves,
176
Blueberry Raspberry Preserves,
175
Cherry Red Raspberry Jam, 33
Peach Preserves with
Raspberries, 166
Peach Raspberry Jam,
No-Sugar, 79
Pear Jam, 32
Pineapple Raspberry Jam with
Apricots, No-Sugar, 83
Preserves, 173
Preserves, Quick, 151
Red and Black Raspberry Jam
with Cherries, 35
Red Currant Preserves, 174
Sauce, 226
Ratatouille Marmalade, 143
Rhubarb
Blackberry Jam, 39
Blueberry Rhubarb Jam, 62
Fig Jam, 27
Ginger Fool, 237
Ginger Jam, 38
Strawberry Rhubarb Jam, 26
ripeness guide for fruits and
vegetables, 251–256
Risen Biscuits, 210
Rosemary Red Onion Jelly, 110

S

Sauce
Blackberry, 207
Blueberry, 220
Fruit, Made from Jams and
Preserves, Master Recipe for,
245
Plum, 208
Raspberry, 226
scale, digital, 6
Scones
Buttermilk Currant, 200
Cream, 199
Drop, 200
Seasonal Guide to Fresh Fruits
and Vegetables for Preserving,
251–256
Serviceberry and Wild Black
Raspberry Jam, 68
Shell, Tart, Pastry, 246
sieve, 14, 16
Simple Syrup, 244
skimming preserves, 16
Sorbets, Fruit, Master Recipe
for, 223
spices, use of in preserves, 14, 15
Spicy
Blueberry Preserves, 161
Cranberry Jam, 54
Grape Jelly, 97
Pink Grapefruit Marmalade, 121
spoon test for jell, 17
sterilizing jars, 9, 11, 15, 16, 18
storing preserves, 16, 18
straining juices, 14
Strawberry
Apple Strawberry Jam,
No-Sugar, 88
Blackberry Jam, 72
Blackberry Preserves, 164
Jam, 25
Jelly Roll, 248
Kiwifruit Jam, 70
Pineapple Jam, No-Sugar, 90
Preserves, 163
Preserves, Quick, 150
Rhubarb Jam, 26
Trifle, 243

stripper tool, 13
sugar, role of in the jell, 6, 10
Sure-Jell®, 10, 19
Syrup, Simple, 244

T

Tart, Jam, 235
Tart Shell Pastry, 246
Tea Brack, 197
thermometer test for jell, 17
thermometers used in preserving,
15
Tomato
Basil Jam, 49
Orange Jam, 51
Prune Jam, 47
Torte, Linzer, 240
Trifle, Strawberry, 243

V

vacuum sealing, 2, 16
Vanilla
Cherry Jam, 34
Lime Vanilla Marmalade, 128
Quick Pink Grapefruit
Marmalade with Vanilla, 117
Strawberry Kiwifruit Jam with
Vanilla, 70
Sugar, 208
vegetable peeler, 13

W

Waffles, Apple Almond, 205
Walnut Apple Pancakes, 204
weighing, scale for, 6
Whole-Wheat English Muffins,
213

Z

zester, 13
Zucchini
Bread, 195
Lemon Zucchini Marmalade
with Basil, 139
Lime Zucchini Marmalade, 138
Orange Zucchini Marmalade,
140
Ratatouille Marmalade, 143